Luan Ferr

Deism
From Philosophy to Spirituality

Copyright
Original Title: **Deism: From Philosophy to Spirituality**
Copyright © 2023, published in 2024 by Luiz Antonio dos Santos ME.

This book examines the origins and development of deistic philosophy, addressing the role of reason, observation of nature and spirituality in the quest to understand the divine. It offers a historical and philosophical perspective on how deism has influenced religious and scientific thought, without promoting specific doctrines or practices.

Second Edition
Second Edition Production Team
Author: Luan Ferr
Proofreader: Virginia Moreira dos Santos
Graphic Design and Layout: Arthur Mendes da Costa
Cover: Anderson Casagrande Neto
Translation: Anselmo Amaral

Publication and Identification
Deism / By Luan Ferr
Booklas Publishing, 2024
Categories: Philosophy / Religion / Body, Mind and Spirit
DDC: 211 - **CDU:** 141.6

Copyright Notice
All rights reserved to:
Booklas Publishing / Luiz Antonio dos Santos ME

This book may not be reproduced, distributed or transmitted, in whole or in part, by any means, electronic or printed, without the express consent of the copyright holder.

Summary

Marcel Dubois 5

Luan Ferr 7

Chapter 1 The Discovery of Deism 8

Chapter 2 The Awakening of Reason 14

Chapter 3 The Foundations of Deistic Reason 17

Chapter 4 The Origins of Deistic Philosophy 23

Chapter 5 The Universe as an Open Book 27

Chapter 6 God as Creator and Observer 30

Chapter 7 The Deist View of God 36

Chapter 8 Nature as Divine Revelation 43

Chapter 9 Reason as a Guide in the Exploration of the Cosmos 52

Chapter 10 Intellectual Freedom in Deism 60

Chapter 11 The Continuous Search for Divine Truth 68

Chapter 12 The Synthesis of Deistic Reason 73

Chapter 13 Science as an Ally in the Search for the Divine 77

Chapter 14 The Deist View of God 85

Chapter 15 The Evolution of Representations of God 91

Chapter 16 The Evolution of Representations of God 99

Chapter 17 The Universality of the Search for God 107

Chapter 18 Understanding God in the Modern Age 115

Chapter 19 Humanity and the Search for God 123

Chapter 20 God as an Expression of the Universal Mystery 130

Chapter 21 The Deist Philosophy in Practice 139

Chapter 22 God Beyond Space and Time 146

Chapter 23 The Nature of the Soul in Deism 152
Chapter 24 Contribution to Human History 156
Chapter 25 Famous Deists 161
Acknowledgements 165

Marcel Dubois

The book we are presenting is the result of an interview our research team conducted with a master deist called Marcel Dubois. Marcel lives in a small village in the French countryside, near Bonaguil Castle, a 15th century medieval fortress located in the commune of Saint-Front-sur-Lémance, in the Lot-et-Garonne department, in the Nouvelle-Aquitaine region of southwest France.

Marcel welcomes us into his home, an old stone building surrounded by a flowery garden. Upon entering the house, we are immediately enveloped by a welcoming and enriching atmosphere. The room where the interview takes place is his personal library, a space with dark oak shelves stretching from floor to ceiling, filled with old books, some with gilded details. The wood of the shelves exudes a soft scent, seeming to evoke the wisdom accumulated in the pages of those many books.

On the walls that aren't lined with shelves, paintings of natural landscapes and portraits of philosophical figures adorn the room. An oil painting of the stunning landscape surrounding his village creates a sense of connection with nature. Another painting, a black and white engraving of Voltaire, the Enlightenment thinker, seems to silently observe the conversation taking place.

Marcel Dubois, the deist master, is dressed simply and elegantly. He wears a white linen shirt, which looks tailored, combined with black wool pants and a navy blue vest. His gray hair is impeccably combed and his clear eyes radiate tranquility and wisdom.

During the interview, Marcel offers us chamomile tea, served in delicate porcelain cups adorned with blue flowers. The tea emits a comforting aroma, which mingles with the smell of old books. The ambient temperature is mild, typical of autumn, with a fireplace burning in one corner of the room, providing the gentle warmth that contrasts with the coolness outside.

This setting, full of elements that evoke nature, erudition and contemplation, provided the perfect environment for the conversation with Marcel Dubois about his faith, his worldview and his teachings.

Luan Ferr

Without reason, God would not exist, for it is through reason that the mind rises to intuit that which transcends its own nature, reason being both the instrument and the receptacle of that which it seeks. However, God, being the very essence of reason, remains beyond the limits of comprehension. Paradoxically, it is only by exercising reason that we conceive of the divine, recognizing that to understand God is ultimately to embrace the mystery of a reason that exceeds reason itself, reason being, like God himself, the beginning and end of all things.

Luan Ferr

Chapter 1
The Discovery of Deism

Marcel Dubois was a young doctor in the city of Avignon, France, when doubts about conventional conceptions of God began to haunt him. He grew up in a devout family, attending church regularly and learning about a God portrayed as a paternal, interventionist figure with human characteristics. As he studied medicine and witnessed people suffering, the traditional image of God began to seem inadequate.

Marcel saw people suffering from incurable diseases, children being born with disabilities and a growing disparity between the rich and the poor. He began to wonder how a benevolent God would allow such suffering and inequality.

As his doubts grew, Marcel turned to conventional religious scriptures for answers, but as he read the texts held sacred, he came across descriptions of a God that left him even more confused. God, in these scenarios, was often portrayed as an anthropomorphic being, with human characteristics, emotions and even preferences. This representation of God as a human figure seemed too simplistic for him.

Marcel's first rational reaction after consulting the scriptures was to conclude that God didn't exist, and that's when something inside him refused to adopt such a perspective. His doubts and disenchantment led him to seek a deeper, more personal understanding of God. He longed for a spiritual connection that wasn't limited by religious dogma or simplistic representations.

As Marcel Dubois continued his search for a deeper understanding of God, he found himself immersed in a sea of religious and spiritual philosophies. He studied the world's religious traditions, explored the theology of different cultures and read extensively about philosophy. Marcel wanted to find a God who was compatible with his intuition, the bearer of a higher power that transcended human limitations.

However, Marcel had not yet found a philosophy that answered all his questions. He wondered about the purpose of existence, the meaning of life and the fate of the soul after death. His questions led him to question the organized religions that didn't have the answers; there was room in him for a broader, freer understanding of God.

Marcel began to explore the works of philosophers who challenged traditional conceptions of God. He was intrigued by the arguments of thinkers who saw God as an impersonal force, an energy that permeated the cosmos. These ideas made him question whether divinity could be more than an entity with a will of its own, but a universal presence that operated according to natural laws.

As he immersed himself in his search, Marcel felt a growing sense that deism, a philosophy that emphasized belief in a transcendent, non-interventionist God immanent in the universe, was more in line with his personal vision. Deism seemed to offer the freedom to explore and develop one's own understanding of God, without the restrictions of conventional religious doctrines.

At this stage of his journey, Marcel began to formulate his own theories about spirituality and God.

The restlessness of Marcel Dubois' soul continued to grow as he delved deeper into his search. His conversations with theologians, readings of sacred texts and exploration of different spiritual currents only increased his desire to understand the divine more fully.

At times, Marcel wondered if humanity had projected its own weaknesses and imperfections onto its conception of God. This led him to consider the possibility that God's true nature was very different, something beyond human comprehension and external to established religions. He felt that divinity could not be reduced to a simple figure with human characteristics.

The vision of a God who does not intervene directly in human affairs, but instead establishes the natural laws that govern the universe, began to make more sense. He saw God as the Creator and Maintainer of the cosmos, whose universal laws allowed life to exist and evolve. This view not only made God more impartial, but also made divine understanding more accessible.

However, Marcel still faced challenges, he wondered about the purpose of life and the fate of the soul after death, questions that continued to disturb him.

As Marcel Dubois progressed in his quest for a clearer understanding of God, he found himself at a crossroads. His persistent doubts about conventional religions and his growing convictions about the divine nature left him in a state of deep reflection.

It was on a rainy afternoon, while exploring his vast collection of books, that he had an encounter that would change the course of his story. Among the many dusty volumes that made up his vast library, he discovered an ancient treatise on deism, written by an 18th century philosopher.

The simplicity and clarity of the text contained in the book resonated deeply with Marcel. He saw deism as the answer to all questions. It was the philosophy that reconciled his search for truth with his understanding of a higher God.

In the days that followed, Marcel immersed himself in reading and studying deism, discovering that this philosophy had been embraced by many of history's greatest thinkers who saw deism as the only way to harmonize reason with spirituality, allowing them to explore divine questions without submitting to religious dogma.

A deep connection was established with this tradition of thought. Marcel realized that deism not only embraced his belief in a transcendent and immanent God, but also encouraged the constant search for truth through reason and observation of the natural world. It was a philosophy that allowed their faith to flourish without the restrictions of traditional religious interpretations, and something very relevant, the history of Deism was untainted.

The discovery of Deism was a moment of spiritual clarity. Marcel began to fully embrace this philosophy, not just as an answer to his own questions, but as a way of sharing his understanding of the divine with others. It was at this point that his spiritual journey transformed him from a seeker into an advocate of deism, and then into a master deist.

Thus, Marcel Dubois found his purpose: to spread the principles of deism, to inspire others to question conventional conceptions of God and to guide those who seek a deeper understanding of the divine Being. His journey of spiritual transformation not only changed his life, but also shaped the destiny of many who shared his wisdom and vision of God. And as he continued to explore the complexities of spirituality and existence, Marcel's legacy as a master deist continued to grow, offering light and inspiration to those seeking answers to their own questions about God and the meaning of life.

Chapter 2
The Awakening of Reason

Long ago, when human beings were searching for answers to the questions surrounding their own existence, a group of sharp-minded thinkers embarked on an intellectual journey that, over time, would blossom into the formation of a philosophy deeply reverent of reason and observation.

In times past, when institutional religions held absolute sway, dictating the lives of individuals through ritual and dogma, dissenting murmurs began to emerge, whispers of questioning that dared to challenge simplistic explanations.

The advent of deism, which rose from the foundations of Renaissance thinkers and the keen minds of the Scientific Revolution, was a response to these dissenting murmurs. As discoveries and advances in astronomy, physics and biology accumulated, these brave souls began to discern an intriguing pattern emerging before their eyes.

It is not, historically, a mere contemplation of distant deities that these early philosophers observed when they cast their gaze to the night skies. Instead, they perceived an unquestionable harmony, like a celestial choreography, in which stars and planets played precise roles. Each orbit proclaimed, in silent testimony, the cosmic harmony.

They turned their gaze to the intrinsic complexity of nature and observed the invariability of natural phenomena. The seasons followed their course with regularity, the rivers flowed obeying the laws of physics, and life unfolded according to patterns that defied randomness. From this meticulous observation, a fundamental question arose: "Is nature itself the vehicle through which God reveals himself?"

Thus, the deist ancestors, pioneers of this philosophy, challenged the traditional narratives and proposed a deeper understanding of divinity. For them, God was not a despotic celestial sovereign who ruled through punishments and rewards, but a Creator who had endowed humanity with a precious gift: reason.

Deism is the philosophy that praises reason as an instrument of knowledge and connection with the transcendental. Reason is conceived as a divine luminescence, present in every human being as a sacred gift. This optional light enables the search for knowledge and the apprehension of the intricate web that constitutes the world around us. In Deism, this luminescence is perceived as a direct link with the Creator, a spark that guides the search for an understanding of the divine.

Deism therefore encourages inquiry, investigation and exploration. It believes that truth is revealed through careful analysis and deep reflection.

Diverging from religions that demand blind faith, Deism is guided by reason as the compass that guides the journey towards the truth.

Deism is thus an invitation to reverent contemplation, recognizing the great order that permeates the universe. Deists interpret natural phenomena as manifestations of divine sagacity. They don't see God as a celestial tyrant, but rather as the Creator who gives humanity the gift of intellectual freedom. Thus, human beings are free to explore the truth and forge their own understanding of the divine based on their own personal quest.

Deism allows us to transcend the limitations of literal interpretations of scripture, embracing instead a deeper and more enlightened understanding of divinity. It is a philosophy that encourages the exploration of nature and God through insightful observation of the natural world and thoughtful reflection.

Chapter 3
The Foundations of Deistic Reason

It is essential to understand that reason is the light that guides us in the darkness. It is the flame that drives us to seek answers to the profound questions that permeate existence. Without reason, we would be lost in the vastness of the unknown, unable to decipher the mysteries of the universe and of God. Without reason, the human race would have gone extinct or would still be living in caves.

In Deism, reason is the foundation that allows us to understand God through careful observation of the world around us. It can be seen as the key that unlocks the secrets of creation. When we contemplate the complexity of nature, when we observe the laws that govern the universe, we are led to a deep appreciation of the divine intelligence that permeates everything.

It's as if reason were a magnifying glass that allows us to see details invisible to the naked eye. It allows us to perceive the order and harmony hidden behind the chaotic appearance of life. It is through reason that we begin to recognize that the universe is not the result of chance, but the result of a creative and intelligent mind.

Reason is the germ of understanding God, the starting point for the spiritual journey. It enables us to question dogmas and unfounded beliefs, encouraging us to explore the natural world with critical eyes and an open mind. As we cultivate our capacity for reason, we begin to see the complexity of creation as an expression of divine wisdom.

Reason, as mentioned, is the beacon that guides us in our exploration of the divine. Now, it will lead us through the infinite universe, revealing how we deists use it as a crucial tool to decipher the patterns and order inherent in creation.

As we contemplate the cosmos, we are immersed in a vastness that defies comprehension. Millions of stars dot the sky, galaxies stretch as far as the eye can see, and unimaginable cosmic phenomena occur billions of light years away. In this environment, it is reason that allows us to begin to understand this grandeur.

We, and when I say we I mean the deists, understand the cosmos as the manifestation of divine intelligence. Each galaxy, each star and each planet play precise roles in a cosmic dance orchestrated by a creative mind. It is through reason that we begin to discern this harmony.

Imagine that reason is like a powerful telescope that allows us to observe details that would otherwise remain invisible. It enables us to study the natural laws that govern the universe, such as gravity, thermodynamics and quantum mechanics, and to recognize in them the mark of divine intelligence.

Through reason, we begin to realize that the cosmos is not random chaos, but an immense cosmic symphony in which each element plays its part according to precise laws. Careful observation of the cosmos leads us to admire the order that permeates the universe, as if each star and galaxy were notes in a score written by God.

In the journey we undertake as deist teachers, reason stands out as an essential tool for discerning divine truth and challenging blind beliefs that often obscure understanding.

As mentioned, dissenting voices have emerged who have refused to accept simplistic explanations. Here, reason stands as an ally in the fight against dogmatic rigidity. We see reason as the antidote to the passive acceptance of inflexible religious dogmas, which often serve only noble purposes.

As we wield reason, we are enabled to question the narratives that have been imposed on us, to challenge predetermined answers and to explore the unknown with intellectual courage.

Deists are not content with superficial explanations. They strive to seek the truth through insightful observation and critical thinking. Reason is their compass, guiding them on their journey in search of divine truth.

When faced with inflexible dogmas, reason invites us to investigate, question and explore beyond the limitations imposed by blind beliefs. It enables us to discern the truth through careful observation, allowing us to distinguish between blind faith and reasoned understanding.

As mentioned earlier, reason is the lens that allows us to observe and understand the world, but it is also seen as the means of direct connection with God, after all, God is only known through reason.

To understand this connection, it is necessary to consider that, in Deism, God is conceived as the great architect of the universe, the one who created the natural laws that govern existence. Reason, in turn, is seen as a divine spark present in every human being, a sacred gift that allows us to seek knowledge and understand the complexity of the world around us. Without reason we would just be irrational animals.

Reason allows us to cross the chasm that separates the human mind from the mind of God. When we contemplate nature and observe the laws that govern the universe, we are, in a way, attuning our mind to the divine mind.

We believe that by using reason to understand the natural world, we are somehow seeking to understand God himself. Every scientific discovery, every careful observation of nature, is seen as a step towards understanding the creative mind behind creation.

To make exploring the role of reason in Deism more enriching, I invite you to take a brief trip back in time, transport yourself to medieval times, when religious dogma was unquestionable, and faith undeniably supplanted reason.

Imagine, for a moment, being in a world where religious beliefs are governed by rigid and inflexible doctrines, where dogmas are accepted without question. Times when current thinking often considered concepts that seem absurd to us today to be true.

At this time, the Earth was widely seen as the center of the universe, with the Sun and the planets revolving around it. The cosmos, however mysterious, was interpreted according to the religious conceptions of the time. Ideas that challenged this view, such as the notion of an infinite and ever-expanding universe or the theory that the earth revolved around the sun and not the other way around, were considered heretical and extremely dangerous.

Imagine how challenging it would be to live in a world where reason is often stifled by the authority of faith and religious institutions. How difficult it would be to question the dogmas that shape our understanding of the universe and existence.

It's important to note that, throughout history, humanity has progressed thanks to the inherent ability to question, to explore the unknown and to challenge simplistic explanations. Thanks to reason, we have freed ourselves from the shackles of dogmatic ignorance and embarked on an intellectual journey in search of the truth. We have made some progress, but Deism invites us to continue the journey, to reflect on the fundamental importance of questioning, investigating and exploring, even when the world around us insists on accepting fabricated explanations.

As we progress through this theme, we will explore in depth the principles of Deism and how reason enables us to understand God and the complexity of existence. I invite you to keep an open mind, embrace critical thinking and move forward on this journey with intellectual courage. For, like those early deists, we are challenged to seek divine truth through reason and insightful observation, even when it means challenging the beliefs that have been bequeathed to us.

Chapter 4
The Origins of Deistic Philosophy

In the Renaissance, Europe witnessed a cultural and intellectual renaissance that would echo down the ages, profoundly marking the history of humanity. This period of intellectual effervescence was a beacon for inquisitive minds, who began to question the traditional conceptions that had prevailed for centuries.

Between the 14th and 16th centuries, the European continent became the epicenter of a cultural revolution, where art, science and philosophy flourished like never before. It was an era of rediscovering the works of classical antiquity, as well as exploring new frontiers of knowledge.

In this cultural renaissance, Renaissance thinkers looked to both the past and the future. They drew inspiration from ancient Greek and Roman ideas, while also exploring the rich cultures of the East. Driven by an insatiable curiosity, they questioned the traditional religious interpretations that had shaped society for centuries.

In this context, humanist philosophy came to the fore. Humanists celebrated humanity's intrinsic capacity for reason and creativity, believing that human beings play an active role in the search for truth. Reason became the guide in understanding the world and spirituality.

Notable figures such as Leonardo da Vinci, who explored the connection between art and science, and Nicolaus Machiavelli, who questioned traditional conceptions of government and power, emerged. These thinkers opened the door to a more open and critical view of the world, a view that, as we shall see, would profoundly influence Deism.

The Scientific Revolution, another crucial milestone in the history of human thought, brought with it remarkable advances in the fields of astronomy, physics and biology. During this period of intellectual effervescence, brilliant minds such as Copernicus, Galileo Galilei and Johannes Kepler revolutionized the understanding of the universe.

These visionaries laid the foundations of modern astronomy, challenging the geocentric view of the universe and asserting that the Earth was not the center of the cosmos, but just a small planet orbiting the Sun. His discoveries were radically innovative, questioning old conceptions that established man as the pinnacle of divine creation.

In the sphere of physics, Isaac Newton emerged as an iconic figure of the Scientific Revolution. His theory of gravity and his laws of motion provided a solid framework for understanding the workings of the universe. The power of reason, together with meticulous observation and critical investigation, was fundamental to his discoveries.

In biology, figures such as Andreas Vesalius and William Harvey advanced the understanding of the human body and blood circulation through anatomical studies and experiments. As new perspectives on life and nature were revealed, observation and experimentation became cornerstones of scientific research.

The Scientific Revolution not only challenged established dogmas, but also elevated reason as a fundamental tool in understanding the natural world. The pioneers of this revolution demonstrated that careful observation and critical investigation were essential to the search for truth. This resonated deeply with Deist philosophy.

As literal interpretations of scripture and traditional dogma were questioned, new horizons opened up for understanding spirituality. In this context of turbulent ideas and religious skepticism, Deism emerged as the philosophy that placed reason at the heart of the search for God.

Deists refused to passively accept conventional religious narratives. Instead, they proposed a profound and rational understanding of the divine. For deists, reason was an ally in the search for spiritual truth, especially when dogmatic truths were falling apart. Deism emerged as a response to the religious skepticism of the time.

This philosophy praises reason as a light that illuminates the path in the darkness of uncertainty, enabling us to discern the truth through meticulous observation and critical thinking. Deism celebrated the search for truth based on reason, as opposed to blind faith. When the fall of one dogma cast suspicion on others, inquisitive minds were encouraged to deeply question the truths established by the dominant faith.

This initial conversation is the start of the journey. As we move forward, we delve deeper into the knowledge and principles of Deism, exploring how reason becomes an ally in understanding God and the complexity of existence. Remain open-minded, embrace critical thinking to continue this journey with intellectual courage, just like those early Deists who dared to challenge the beliefs bequeathed to them.

Chapter 5
The Universe as an Open Book

To understand this connection, it is necessary to consider that, in Deism, God is conceived as the great architect of the universe, the one who created the natural laws that govern existence. Reason, in turn, is seen as a divine spark present in every human being, a sacred gift that allows us to seek knowledge and understand the complexity of the world around us. Without reason, we would just be irrational animals.

Reason allows us to cross the chasm that separates the human mind from the mind of God. When we contemplate nature and observe the laws that govern the universe, we are, in a way, attuning our mind to the divine mind.

We believe that by using reason to understand the natural world, we are somehow seeking to understand God himself. Every scientific discovery, every careful observation of nature, is seen as a step towards understanding the creative mind behind creation.

To make exploring the role of reason in Deism more enriching, I invite you to take a brief trip back in time, transport yourself to medieval times, when religious dogma was unquestionable, and faith undeniably supplanted reason.

Imagine, for a moment, being in a world where religious beliefs are governed by rigid and inflexible doctrines, where dogmas are accepted without question. Times when current thinking often considered concepts that seem absurd to us today to be true.

At this time, the Earth was widely seen as the center of the universe, with the Sun and the planets revolving around it. The cosmos, however mysterious, was interpreted according to the religious conceptions of the time. Ideas that challenged this view, such as the notion of an infinite and ever-expanding universe or the theory that the Earth revolved around the sun and not the other way around, were considered heretical and extremely dangerous.

Imagine how challenging it would be to live in a world where reason is often stifled by the authority of faith and religious institutions. How difficult it would be to question the dogmas that shape our understanding of the universe and existence.

It's important to note that, throughout history, humanity has progressed thanks to the inherent ability to question, to explore the unknown and to challenge simplistic explanations. Thanks to reason, we have freed ourselves from the shackles of dogmatic ignorance and embarked on an intellectual journey in search of the truth. We have made some progress, but Deism invites us to continue the journey, to reflect on the fundamental importance of questioning, investigating and exploring, even when the world around us insists on accepting fabricated explanations.

As we progress through this theme, we will explore in depth the principles of Deism and how reason enables us to understand God and the complexity of existence. I invite you to keep an open mind, embrace critical thinking and move forward on this journey with intellectual courage. For, like those early deists, we are challenged to seek divine truth through reason and insightful observation, even when it means challenging the beliefs that have been bequeathed to us.

Chapter 6
God as Creator and Observer

We contemplate God as the Master Creator, the one who skillfully shaped the universe and established its intrinsic order and harmony. This perception of God as a divine craftsman is fundamental to understanding the core of deistic philosophy.

We conceive of God as the supreme craftsman, the one who meticulously planned every detail of creation. In this view, God is the supreme architect who designed the universe, defining natural laws and principles that govern all things.

This conception of God as a Divine Craftsman differs substantially from traditional conceptions of divinity. While many religions portray God as a personal and interventionist being, we see God as the great creator who, after creating the universe, allows it to take its natural course, without direct intervention. After all, an interventionist God would balance the existential scales, and everyone would share the same living conditions, including health, family and resources. The difference in the unequal distribution of the means that provide existential fulfillment would be the explanation that would prove that the Deist doctrine is the most appropriate for understanding God.

This fundamental difference in the vision of God is one of the distinctive characteristics of Deism. We believe that God has given humanity the gift of reason and free inquiry to understand creation, rather than relying exclusively on divine revelation or the interpretation of others. Deistic philosophy therefore values and respects the human capacity to observe, reflect and understand the world on the basis of reason.

We see God as the Creator who gave humanity the gift of intellectual autonomy. Rather than imposing his will directly, God is perceived as the one who entrusted humanity with the responsibility of exploring and understanding creation through careful observation and critical thinking. It is as if God had written the "score" of the universe, and humanity was free to "play" the music of truth through reason.

This view of God as a Divine Artificer not only influenced deistic philosophy, but also challenged traditional religious narratives that emphasized constant divine intervention in human life.

God as the Great Architect of the universe is a metaphor often used by deists to describe the vision of

God as Creator. This representation of God further highlights the precision and order inherent in creation, emphasizing the meticulous planning role He plays in the design of the universe.

In this vision, God is the one who defined the rules of the cosmic game, establishing the physics, chemistry and natural laws that govern the functioning of the whole. Every phenomenon, from the movement of planets to the formation of molecules, is the result of God's ingenuity in creating an interconnected and harmonious system.

The metaphor of the Great Architect highlights the precision and order present in creation, showing how God designed a universe full of complexity and beauty. We see nature itself as the result of this divine planning, where each being and each element plays a precise role in the choreography of existence.

This conception of God as the Great Architect also highlights the autonomy of creation. Just as an architect designs a bridge so that it can support its own weight, God designed the universe with the intrinsic capacity to function in a self-sustaining way. We believe that God doesn't need to intervene constantly, because he has already established the laws and principles that govern everything.

This vision of God as the Great Architect not only emphasizes the order and precision present in creation, but also highlights the importance of human reason in the search for divine understanding. We believe that careful observation of the world around us, combined with critical thinking, is fundamental to uncovering God's plan for the human race.

The metaphor of the Great Architect is a powerful representation of God's vision, emphasizing the beauty, complexity and harmony of the universe, as well as the importance of human reason in exploring this divine creation.

In Deism, God is a Benevolent Observer, and this perspective goes beyond divine creation to God's continuous observation and care for the universe. God not only gave birth to the universe, but also observes it with care and compassion, taking an active interest in everything that happens within creation.

We see God as the one who closely follows the development of life, the evolution of the stars and the interaction of natural forces. This view reflects the belief that God is benevolent and desires the well-being of his creation.

The conception of God as a Benevolent Observer profoundly influences deist philosophy, promoting the idea that order and harmony in the universe are a reflection of divine wisdom. We deists see the complexity and interconnectedness of all things as evidence of God's care in creating a system that allows life to flourish and prosper.

This view also highlights the importance of human reason in the search for divine understanding. Just as God carefully observes his creation, humanity is called to observe and understand the world with a critical mind and a compassionate heart. Through reason, human beings can seek divine wisdom in the order and beauty of the universe.

The notion of a Benevolent Observer God is a source of inspiration and hope. Creation is a precious gift from God, full of wonders to be explored and understood. This vision strengthens the conviction that the search for knowledge and truth is a spiritual journey that brings us closer to God.

Therefore, the vision of God as a Benevolent Observer is a fundamental part of deistic philosophy, highlighting God's compassion and continuous interest in his creation, as well as the importance of human reason in the search for divine understanding, cosmic order and harmony in nature are crucial elements that reflect God's divine intelligence and wisdom.

We see the precision of planetary orbits, the regularity of the seasons and the laws of physics that govern the universe as clear evidence of the intelligence of a Creator. Each of these elements, when observed carefully, reveals a meticulous plan and an order that transcends chance.

The order and harmony present in nature are interpreted as a testimony to God's wisdom. We believe that God established the natural laws and principles that govern the universe, thus creating an environment conducive to life and evolution. This view emphasizes that the natural world is not chaotic, but an expression of the divine mind.

The cosmic order and harmony in nature inspire us to contemplate God's wisdom and to seek a deeper connection with the divine. We see beauty in the simplicity of natural laws and in the complexity of the interactions between living beings and the environment. Every aspect of creation is seen as a manifestation of a greater creative intelligence.

This understanding of order and harmony in the universe is a central theme of our philosophy. It highlights the importance of reason as a tool for observing and understanding natural laws, as we believe that by exploring and studying the natural world with an open and critical mind, human beings can more deeply uncover the all-pervading wisdom of God.

Chapter 7
The Deist View of God

In the deist's journey in search of divine understanding, the conception of God plays a central and transcendental role. As we delve into the depths of deism, it is essential to understand the unique view that deistic teachers have of God.

Deists believe that God is an immaterial entity, devoid of physical form. This belief contrasts with many religions that portray deities as anthropomorphic beings. For deists, God is a spiritual presence that permeates the universe, being both the primordial source of all things and the essence that transcends all forms. This immaterial vision of God invites deists to connect with divinity in a unique way, devoid of rituals and dogmas, seeking a more personal understanding.

In addition to his immaterial nature, deists see God as a transcendental entity. This means that God is beyond human comprehension and cannot be limited by human concepts. Deists believe that God's transcendence is what makes possible the existence of the universe and the natural order that governs it. God is seen as the supreme architect who established the laws of the universe and allowed life to flourish according to these laws, but this God does not intervene directly in human affairs.

The deist view of God invites followers to contemplate the mystery of existence and to seek divine understanding through reason and observation of their surroundings. For deists, the search for knowledge of God is a personal and continuous journey, an intellectual and spiritual exploration that challenges the mind and nourishes the soul. In the process, deists strive to understand the purpose of life and the connection between human existence and the divine plan.

Deism, with its immaterial and transcendental vision of God, transcends religious and cultural barriers. It offers a universal philosophy that invites everyone to explore the nature of divinity in a way that respects the diversity of beliefs and their perspectives. While many traditional religions have specific representations of God, deists celebrate the simplicity and universality of their vision, inviting individuals to find the sacred in the world around them and within themselves.

To understand the deist way of seeing God, it is essential to unravel the anthropomorphic representations that often dominate traditional religious conceptions. Deists, by rejecting the idea of a God with a human form or any other form that religions represent, challenge the limitations of the human mind, inviting everyone to transcend the common images associated with divinity.

In many religions, God is often portrayed with human characteristics, such as a face, arms, legs and emotional attributes. This anthropomorphization of God makes him more accessible to people, allowing them to relate to a divine figure who seems understandable and close. However, deists argue that this approach reduces the divine nature and puts God in a box limited by human imagination.

In this context, it is imperative to clarify that any plastic figure, which the human mind tries to reproduce the image of God, cannot be conceived by even the most modest minds. It is well known that the human form was a biological adaptation necessary for the survival of the species and that this form was perfected over time to adjust to the needs of natural evolution. It is incomprehensible that the rational human mind should imagine that an immaterial being, who did not need to undergo biological adaptations, would have this same form.

Deists believe that the representation of God as an anthropomorphic entity is a limitation that prevents a true understanding of God. They argue that God is beyond comprehension and by trying to portray Him with human characteristics, we run the risk of limiting

His greatness and transcendence. For deists, God is such a vast and complex entity that the mind cannot conceive of Him in completeness.

By rejecting anthropomorphic representations, deists invite seekers to look beyond conventional images of God and explore the true nature of divinity. They emphasize that understanding God must be based on reason, observation of the natural order and the continuous search for divine knowledge. This search for the true nature of God is an intellectual and spiritual journey that challenges the mind and expands the horizons of human understanding.

Deists believe that the universe is a manifestation of the divine will of an immaterial and transcendental God. Instead of God being an active figure who constantly interferes in creation, He is the creator who established the natural laws that govern everything. This point of view invites deists to contemplate the order and complexity of the universe as evidence of divine wisdom.

For deists, God's immaterial nature emphasizes the simplicity and universality of divinity. Instead of adopting complex mythologies or religious dogmas, deists find beauty in the simplicity of their vision of God as the primordial cause of all that exists. This inspires them to appreciate creation in its purest form, recognizing God's presence in the harmony of the natural world.

Deists see God's immaterial and transcendental nature as an invitation to human responsibility in preserving and caring for creation. We believe that, as rational beings, we have a duty to act ethically and morally to protect the environment and promote harmony. Understanding divinity as transcendental reminds us that we are part of a greater order and that our connection with God is reflected in our actions.

As we explore the deistic view of God, it is crucial to understand how this conception of God's immaterial and transcendental nature relates to human life and the spiritual journey. Deists believe that this unique view of divinity has profound implications for the understanding of the soul, human existence and the path towards divine knowledge.

In deism, the human soul is seen as a divine spark, a part of God's transcendental essence. This view rooted in the immaterial nature of God highlights the idea that each individual carries with them an intrinsic connection with the divine. The soul is perceived as immortal, not subject to physical death, and its journey is linked to the search for an understanding of God and spiritual evolution.

For deists, the search for divine knowledge is a personal and intellectual journey that involves the exploration of one's own soul. We believe that by cultivating reason, ethics and contemplation, individuals can get closer to God. The transcendental nature of God serves as an inspiration for this continuous search, encouraging deists to deepen their understanding of divinity and the universe.

Deists emphasize the importance of ethics as an integral part of the spiritual journey. They believe that understanding morality is linked to understanding the divine will and recognizing human responsibility in preserving balance and harmony in the world. This connection between ethics and spirituality is an essential part of the deist view of God's transcendental nature.

Deists see the evolution of the soul as a continuous process of spiritual improvement. They believe that, as the soul seeks divine knowledge and a deeper connection with God, it advances towards transcendence. The soul is seen as an essential part of the divine plan, destined to return to unity with God after its journey of spiritual search and evolution.

For deists, the understanding of God as an immaterial and transcendental entity is a call to contemplation. This contemplation is not limited to specific religious rituals, but rather to an intellectual and spiritual quest that invites individuals to meditate on the nature of the universe and their relationship with God. It is a call to deepen the spiritual connection through reflection and the search for divine knowledge.

The deist view of the soul as a divine spark that seeks to evolve towards transcendence leads to the intrinsic desire to achieve unity with the creator. Deists believe that, throughout its spiritual journey, the soul draws ever closer to divinity, transcending the limitations of human existence and returning to unity with the transcendental. This search for unity with God is the ultimate goal of a deist's spiritual journey.

The experience of unity with God is considered a state of profound spiritual communion. Deists believe that, on reaching this state, the soul attains a complete understanding of divinity and experiences a sense of peace, harmony and fulfillment. It is the ultimate fulfillment of the quest for divine knowledge and represents the consummation of the spiritual journey.

However, deists also recognize that the quest for divine knowledge and unity with God is an ongoing journey. It is not a destination, but a constant process of spiritual improvement and reflection. Deists are called to continue deepening their understanding of divinity and to seek unity with God throughout their lives.

Chapter 8
Nature as Divine Revelation

As deists, we see nature as an open book, a divine text written in the language of natural patterns. Every phenomenon, every form and every cycle of life are words that reveal the divine wisdom behind creation. Careful observation of these natural patterns is essential to deciphering this language and understanding the intelligence that permeates all existence.

Our critical and contemplative gaze on the cycles of life allows us to glimpse the precision with which God planned nature. By observing the journey of a seed that grows into a majestic tree, we understand that each stage of this process reveals a divine purpose. Deists see this cycle of life as the manifestation of creation and the continuity of nature's wonders.

Furthermore, we find in the symmetry of natural forms a clear indication of God's wisdom. Symmetry is a universal language that transcends cultural and geographical barriers and is present throughout creation.

From the symmetry of a flower's petals to the geometric perfection of ice crystals, we perceive the divine hand that shapes every detail of nature with precision and harmony.

The harmony of ecosystems is striking evidence of divine intelligence. Every living thing, from tiny ants to majestic eagles, plays a vital role in the interconnection of ecosystems. Everyone's survival is intrinsically linked to the harmony of these natural systems. This leads us to believe that God designed nature in an interdependent way, revealing His wisdom in the complexity of ecological relationships.

Therefore, for us, the attentive and respectful observation of natural patterns is an act of worship and contemplation. Through this coded language, we find the words that bring us closer to God. By deciphering these patterns, we come closer to a deeper understanding of divine intelligence. It's as if each careful observation were a line in a poem, and our task is to read with reverence and humility, seeking to unlock the secrets that God has written in nature.

For deists, careful observation of natural patterns not only reveals divine wisdom, but also allows us to perceive the profound unity underlying the diversity of nature. Every living thing, from the tiny creatures that inhabit the most secret corners of the Earth to the majestic trees that touch the heavens, is an interconnected part of a greater whole. This interconnectedness reflects the harmony of the universe and acts as proof of the creative intelligence that permeates all things.

Imagine the diversity of life forms we find on our planet. Each species, from insects to mammals, has unique characteristics and performs specific functions in its ecosystem. However, we see this diversity as a reflection of the richness of the divine plan. Instead of chaos, we find order; instead of randomness, we discover purpose.

Unity in diversity becomes evident when we consider how the different elements of nature complement each other. Plants, for example, carry out photosynthesis, producing oxygen that is vital for animals to breathe. Pollinators, such as bees, play a fundamental role in fertilizing plants, enabling the production of fruit and seeds that serve as food for various species. These complex interactions demonstrate the mutual dependence that exists between living beings and natural elements.

Even atmospheric phenomena such as rainfall are interconnected with life on Earth. Rainfall provides essential water for the survival of all forms of life, from plants to human beings. The way water is distributed and recycled in nature is an example of the harmony that sustains ecological balance.

This underlying unity in the diversity of nature is seen by deists as a manifestation of God's creative intelligence. Instead of a Creator who built each element of creation in isolation, we see God as the Master Architect who designed an interconnected and harmonious system, where all parts play a vital role in the choreography of existence.

We deists pay deep reverence to the complexity and interdependence of all things. Each organism, each natural element and each atmospheric phenomenon are like notes in a divine symphony, contributing to the harmony of the universe. This understanding inspires us to care for and preserve the diversity of nature, recognizing that damage to any one part affects the beauty and integrity of the whole. Unity in diversity is, for us, a powerful lesson in the intelligence and order that govern the universe.

For deists, nature acts as a mirror that reflects divinity, and this perspective invites us to contemplate the elements of nature as reflections of God's intelligence. Careful observation of nature is more than mere aesthetic appreciation; it is a search for a deeper understanding of the divine. We believe that by examining nature with attentive eyes, we find indications of God's presence and wisdom in all things.

Imagine yourself in a natural setting, in an environment untouched by human influence. You observe the majestic mountains, the constantly flowing rivers, the ancient trees that rise to touch the sky and the creatures that inhabit this landscape. For us, each of these elements is a mirror that reflects divinity in a unique way.

The mountains, with their unchanging solidity throughout the ages, remind us of God's stability and constancy. The rivers, with their incessant flow, represent the fluidity of life and the constant renewal that takes place in the universe. The trees, which serve as a habitat and food source for countless creatures, show us the generosity and interconnectedness that permeates creation. The creatures that inhabit this environment display an incredible diversity of forms and functions, highlighting God's infinite creativity.

Contemplation of nature is not just a passive appreciation; it is an active search for understanding. Deists see the order and beauty present in nature as manifestations of divine intelligence. Every pattern, cycle and relationship in nature is a clue that helps us unravel the mysteries of creation.

This perspective leads us to seek the divine not only in temples built by human hands, but also in the natural temples around us. For us, nature is an open book, full of lessons about God's presence and wisdom. With every observation, every moment of contemplation, we get a little closer to God.

The fundamental idea is that, when we look at nature, we find much more than just physical elements; we find a spiritual connection with the divine. We believe that God constantly reveals himself through creation, inviting us to delve deeper into understanding the cosmos and God's role as the Master Creator and Benevolent Observer. Therefore, for us, nature is more than a mere backdrop; it is a mirror that reflects divinity in all its aspects, inviting us to a continuous search for spiritual truth.

For deists, reason plays a fundamental role in interpreting nature as divine revelation. We see reason as the lantern that lights the way in the exploration of natural wonders, allowing us to unravel the mysteries of creation and thus reveal God's intelligence behind it all.

Imagine you are in a lush forest, surrounded by the vastness of nature. In front of you is a winding stream, with crystal-clear waters that reflect the sunlight. As you observe this scenery, your mind begins to ask questions. Why does the stream follow this particular course? How does the water flow so smoothly? What is the purpose of the plants and animals that inhabit this environment?

These questions are the result of reason in action. Deists believe that reason is the tool that enables us to ask these questions and seek answers through insightful observation of the natural world. It enables us to examine the patterns, cycles and interactions that occur in nature and to recognize the underlying order.

The application of reason helps us to unravel the mysteries of creation, revealing God's intelligence behind everything. When we contemplate the workings of the stars and planets in the cosmos, the complexity of the ecology of a natural habitat or the intricate structure of a cell, we are applying reason to understand how these elements fit into a greater whole.

Reason also allows us to appreciate the beauty of nature in a deeper way. When we understand the complexity behind a natural phenomenon, our admiration intensifies, as we realize that we are witnessing the masterpiece of an intelligent Creator.

For deists, reason is not an enemy of spirituality, but a valuable ally. Through reason, we are able to seek truth, wisdom and a deep understanding of the divine in creation. It invites us to explore the natural world with an open and curious mind, to ask questions and seek answers based on careful observation and critical reflection.

Therefore, reason plays a central role in the deists' journey to understand nature as divine revelation. It is the light that illuminates the path, enabling us to decipher the language of natural patterns, to perceive unity in nature's diversity and to contemplate nature as a mirror reflecting God. Through the application of reason, we continue our quest to understand the divine intelligence that permeates all things in creation.

As we contemplate nature as divine revelation, we are reminded that we stand before an open holy book, whose pages are filled with wonders and secrets that bring us closer to the Creator. Every careful observation, every question asked by reason and every moment of contemplation leads us on a spiritual journey in search of truth and understanding of the divine intelligence that weaves the tapestry of existence.

Science has corroborated this link between contact with nature and human well-being. Psychological studies have shown that exposure to nature reduces stress and anxiety, improves mood and promotes a sense of relaxation. Forest therapy, known as "shinrin-yoku" in Japan, is a notable example of this phenomenon, associated with significant mental health benefits.

In addition, research indicates that time spent in natural environments is linked to increased creativity, concentration and problem-solving ability. The theory of "attention restoration" suggests that nature provides an environment that allows the brain to rest and revitalize itself, improving the ability to face the challenges of everyday life.

Studies into "nature deficit syndrome" also show that distancing oneself from outdoor activities and exposure to nature can contribute to mental health problems, especially in children. The link between contact with nature and mental health is so powerful that many experts recommend that people integrate more time outdoors into their daily routines.

As a result, we realize that the Deistic view of nature manifests itself intrinsically, as the grandeur of God's creation transcends a complete understanding of Deism. Even those who are not familiar with the principles of Deism somehow feel a deep connection with nature, seeking refuge and peace in it. People walk serene paths, set up camp by rivers or in the middle of forests, take refuge in cozy farm hotels and take their children to play in parks. It's as if, subconsciously, human beings are programmed to seek God where His presence is most easily perceived and felt.

Therefore, in this encounter with nature, the human being not only follows an innate programming, but also enjoys the scientifically proven benefits for mental health, emotional well-being and quality of life. It is a testimony to the intrinsic harmony between divine creation and the human search for peace and spiritual connection.

Chapter 9
Reason as a Guide in the Exploration of the Cosmos

The exploration of the universe has always enchanted the human mind. The desire to understand the secrets of the universe, from the vastness of space to the minutiae of the laws that govern it, has been one of the noblest and most challenging pursuits.

Observing the stars serves as our starting point in the search for answers. Thanks to reason, we have developed telescopes capable of peer deeply into the starry sky. These marvels of engineering allow us to glimpse inconceivable distances and contemplate distant galaxies. Through systematic observation and analysis, astronomers are able to map the structure of the universe, identify stars, planets, asteroids and comets, and trace the trajectory of celestial bodies.

Reason, however, transcends mere observation. It enables us to ask essential questions about the cosmos. Why does the universe exist? How did it begin? These questions instigate the human mind to seek answers, driving scientific and philosophical investigation.

In this context, reason leads us to recognize the profound complexity of the universe and encourages us to decipher its fundamental laws. Mathematics, as a universal language, is an instrument of reason that allows us to describe the precise relationships between celestial phenomena. Scientific theories, such as Einstein's theory of relativity (an avowed Deist) and the big bang theory, are products of human reason that help us understand the universe on macroscopic and microscopic scales.

Space exploration, fueled by reason and curiosity, represents another milestone in the quest to unlock celestial secrets. Humans have built probes and spacecraft that travel to distant planets such as Mars, Jupiter and Saturn, collecting crucial data about these alien worlds. By analyzing this information, we expand our knowledge of planetary composition, atmosphere, geology and the possibility of extraterrestrial life.

In addition, reason allows us to explore the laws that govern the universe at its most fundamental level. Theoretical physics, for example, seeks to understand the nature of matter, energy and the fundamental forces that govern everything that exists. Through experiments, mathematical equations and computer modeling, scientists continue to unravel the mysteries of quantum mechanics, relativity, gravity and other forces that shape the cosmos.

The search for our place in the vast universe is a journey that reason invites us to undertake. It pushes us to question our origin, purpose and connection to the universe, leading us to explore the complexities of human existence in relation to outer space.

Reason encourages us to investigate our own cosmic history. Through scientific studies and discoveries, we begin to understand that the chemical elements that make up our bodies, such as carbon, oxygen and iron, were forged in the depths of the stars. We are, in fact, children of the stars, made of the same materials that shine in the night sky. This understanding connects us in a profound way with the cosmos, making us question our relationship with the universe and how our existence is intrinsically linked to it.

In addition, reason leads us to explore the concept of habitability on other planets. The search for exoplanets, worlds beyond our solar system, is fueled by the desire to find other places where life can exist. This leads us to ponder the possibility of extraterrestrial life and our place in a universe potentially populated by other civilizations. Reason encourages us to consider the philosophical, ethical and scientific implications of this search.

The search for our place in the stars also leads us to question our purpose in the great cosmic tapestry. We reflect on why we are here, what the meaning of our lives is and how we contribute to understanding and preserving the universe. These transcendental questions lead to philosophy and the search for a purpose that transcends our earthly existence.

We are driven to explore space and investigate the unknown in the hope of finding answers to deeper questions. Space missions, such as the exploration of Mars and the search for habitable planets, represent the active search for our place in the stars. Through these endeavors, we come closer to understanding our cosmic origin, our purpose in the universe and our connection with other forms of life.

Space exploration is undoubtedly one of the most impressive manifestations of the human capacity to apply reason in the search for knowledge. As the frontiers of exploration expand beyond the confines of the Earth, we are reminded of the grandeur of the universe and the central role of reason in this endeavor.

Reason, as a tool for questioning and discovery, drives space exploration. From the dawn of astronomy to the present day, humanity has been observing the stars with curious eyes and an analytical mind. Astronomers and scientists study the movements of planets, the orbit of stars and the formation of galaxies, unraveling the mysteries of the universe.

Space exploration is a natural extension of this desire to understand the cosmos. Through space missions, advanced telescopes and interplanetary probes, reason makes it possible to investigate celestial bodies more closely than ever before. We have discovered icy moons, volcanoes on other worlds, storms on gas giants and even signs of water on Mars, all thanks to the application of reason in space exploration.

However, space exploration is not just about collecting data. It also allows us to contemplate the grandeur of the cosmos and our position in it. When we see images of the Earth from space, we are confronted with the fragility and beauty of our planet. This unique perspective reminds us of the importance of caring for our common home and preserving the environment.

In addition, space exploration challenges us to think beyond terrestrial limits. When humans first set foot on the moon, it was a monumental feat of human reason and ingenuity. It inspires us to think about our own limitations and to consider what more we can achieve when we use reason as an ally.

Space exploration is a demonstration of the constant search for knowledge and understanding of the unknown. It is a testament to human determination to overcome seemingly insurmountable challenges, to employ reason to solve complex problems and to explore the mysteries of the universe. Each space mission is an expression of the human desire to broaden horizons and seek answers to the deepest questions about the universe and existence itself.

The intersection between science and cosmic spirituality is a fertile field for the application of human reason. While science seeks to understand the universe through observation and the scientific method, cosmic spirituality explores the connection between human beings and the cosmos from a more transcendental perspective. Reason plays a crucial role in helping us understand how these two paths intertwine and enrich our understanding of the universe and our place in it.

Science, with its objective and methodological approach, provides a detailed and accurate view of the universe. Astronomers and physicists, using telescopes and advanced instruments, study the structure of space-time, the formation of stars and galaxies, and the fundamental processes that govern everything. Reason is the light that guides these scientists, allowing them to decipher the secrets of the cosmos, such as Einstein's theory of relativity (a notorious Deist) and the Big Bang theory.

Cosmic spirituality, on the other hand, seeks to understand the deeper meaning and connection between human beings and the cosmos. For many, contemplating the stars and the vastness of the universe evokes a sense of awe and reverence that transcends scientific understanding. Reason helps to explore these questions, allowing reflection on how our existence is intrinsically linked to the universe and the cosmic order.

The intersection between science and spirituality becomes evident when we recognize that the search for truth in both areas can coexist harmoniously. Many scientists and philosophers, inspired by the wonder of the universe, find meaning and spirituality in exploring the cosmos. The application of reason leads us to question not only the "how" of natural laws, but also the "why" behind them.

Reason also allows us to recognize that science and spirituality are not mutually exclusive, but complementary. A scientific understanding of the universe does not invalidate the spiritual search for meaning and purpose. Instead, they intertwine, offering a more complete and enriching view of the cosmos.

In this context, reason encourages us to embrace the complexity and diversity of perspectives on the universe. It encourages us to keep an open mind to scientific discoveries and to the depths of spirituality. In doing so, we are able to build a deeper and more meaningful understanding of the cosmos and our place in it.

The intersection between science and spirituality is a reminder that human reason can illuminate different facets of the same reality. As we continue to explore the cosmos, guided by the light of reason, we can find answers in both the objective world of science and the subjective world of spirituality. This integration enriches us as human beings, allowing us to contemplate the mystery and majesty of the universe in a more complete and profound way.

In concluding this chapter on the role of reason in understanding the cosmos, it is intriguing to note that one of the most notorious personalities in the history of science, Albert Einstein, professed the Deist faith. Einstein, whose theory of relativity revolutionized the understanding of space and time, saw the universe as a testimony to the order and elegance that human reason could unravel. He believed that only Deism suited his spirituality, because it was only through Deism that he could see God.

Chapter 10
Intellectual Freedom in Deism

In the journey of Deism, intellectual freedom assumes a prominent role, being not only a virtue, but a fundamental pillar that supports the understanding of God and the universe. Deism, as a religious philosophy, stands out for the way it allows individuals to approach the truth independently, exercising the faculty of reason.

From its beginnings, Deism has been shaped by a deep respect for reason. We believe that the human mind is endowed with the innate capacity for discernment, a spark of divinity that allows us to seek the truth in a logical and coherent manner. This belief in the primacy of reason is at the heart of our approach to intellectual freedom.

In Deism, intellectual freedom begins with the freedom to question. We not only allow, but also encourage deep inquiry into the mysteries of the universe and human existence. Questioning is the basis of intellectual progress, and it is through questioning that we begin to unveil the veils that conceal divine truth.

Our intellectual freedom also extends to the freedom to investigate. We encourage individuals to explore, research and acquire knowledge through observation, study and critical analysis. Science and philosophy, as instruments of reason, are valuable allies in the search for truth. We don't see these disciplines as threats to faith, but as complements that enrich our understanding of God.

However, intellectual freedom in Deism is not a solitary journey, but a collective search for truth. We value the exchange of ideas, respectful dialog and the sharing of knowledge. Through healthy debate and open discussion, we improve our understanding and help others find their own path in the search for truth.

Our philosophy of intellectual freedom is also reflected in our attitude towards Scripture and religious traditions. In Deism, we believe that no scripture or tradition should be dogmatically imposed. Instead, we invite individuals to examine these sources of wisdom with the light of reason, exploring them critically in search of the universal truths they may contain.

Importantly, our intellectual freedom is not limited to the religious sphere, but extends to all aspects of life. We believe that reason should guide our ethical, political and social choices, allowing us to make informed and fair decisions. In doing so, we contribute to a more conscious and compassionate world.

Intellectual freedom in Deism is not only a right, but also a responsibility. Through it, each individual is called upon to actively seek the truth, to understand the divine and to contribute to the well-being of humanity. It is a journey of self-discovery, spiritual growth and contribution to a more enlightened world.

Reason plays a central role in the search for truth in Deism, enabling Deists to question established religious concepts and dogmas. We believe that reason is the most valuable tool we have for understanding God and unraveling the mysteries of the universe.

In Deism, we see reason as a divine gift, a faculty that separates us from irrational beings. While animals operate mainly on instinct, human beings have the ability to reason, question and seek answers. It is through this ability to reason that we begin to plumb the depths of existence and question the meaning of life.

Reason allows us to critically evaluate the religious beliefs and teachings presented to us. In Deism, we don't accept dogma without question. Instead, we use reason as a beacon to discern truth from superstition, reality from mythology and wisdom from tradition. We believe that if God has given us the ability to reason, He wants us to use it to seek the truth, including about Himself.

This approach of reason as a guide in the search for divine truth also extends to the interpretation of

Scripture and religious traditions. While many religions insist on literalist interpretations of their sacred texts, in Deism, we use reason to examine these texts critically and contextually. We recognize that the Scriptures can contain symbolic and allegorical meanings, and reason helps us to discern these meanings more deeply.

A fundamental aspect of the role of reason in Deism is the idea that only reason can lead us to the knowledge of God. We know that irrational beings, devoid of the ability to question and reason, cannot understand the nature of God. Reason is the means by which we approach the creator, examining the evidence of creation and seeking to understand the order and harmony of the universe. There is no point in seeking God by simply accepting, without question, dogmas imposed by religious ideologies.

By questioning and exploring with the help of reason, deists have the opportunity to forge a personal connection with God. Instead of blindly accepting religious beliefs, we are challenged to seek our own understanding of the Creator. This journey of spiritual self-discovery is enriched by the ability to reason independently and the freedom to question established religious concepts.

Intellectual freedom in Deism, combined with reason, enables us to explore the depths of divine knowledge, without the restrictions of dogmas and rigid doctrines. It is a journey that invites us to question, to seek answers and to grow in our understanding of God.

Deism, as a philosophy of seeking truth through reason, promotes religious freedom and respect for the diversity of beliefs. At the heart of Deism is the recognition that the spiritual quest is a personal journey and that each individual has the right to follow their own path.

Religious freedom in Deism is seen as an essential value. We believe that forcing the acceptance of religious beliefs or doctrines is counterproductive and detrimental to the true search for divine understanding.

Deists value the diversity of religious perspectives and recognize that different spiritual traditions offer unique approaches to understanding the divine. Rather than rejecting or condemning other beliefs, Deism invites an approach of respect and inter-religious dialogue.

Religious pluralism in Deism is a natural extension of religious freedom. We believe that all religious traditions have something to contribute to our understanding of God. Therefore, we are open to learning from diverse spiritual beliefs and philosophies.

Reason plays a crucial role in promoting this religious pluralism and respect. It is reason that allows us to critically evaluate our own beliefs and be willing to consider other perspectives. Through the exercise of reason, we can discern the truth between different religious beliefs and find points of convergence between them.

Deism recognizes that while religious beliefs may differ, they often share a common desire to understand God and seek a greater purpose in life. This shared understanding can serve as a starting point for interfaith dialogue and cooperation on ethical and moral issues.

Religious freedom and pluralism in Deism also extend to the political sphere. Deists have historically supported the separation of church and state, defending each person's right to their own freedom of conscience and religion. This view aligns with the idea that spiritual pursuit should be a personal choice, not imposed by government or institutions.

Deism is, by nature, a philosophy that values the continuous search for truth. It invites us to explore the universe and understand God through reason, observation and questioning. At the heart of Deism is the idea that truth is not an end point, but a constant journey of discovery and self-discovery. Intellectual freedom in Deism allows us to embrace this journey without fear, and reason is the light that guides us in this incessant search for divine knowledge.

Encouraged by Deism, we are reminded that truth is not a static entity, but a river in constant flow. Through reason, we are enabled to navigate this river, to explore its curves and currents, to dive into its depths and reach new shores. Every question, every investigation, every discovery is a step forward.

In Deism, the search for truth is an expression of our intellectual freedom. We are free to question, challenge, reflect and explore. We are not bound by inflexible dogmas or limitations imposed by religious authorities. Reason is our compass, and freedom is our traveling companion.

By embracing Deism as a philosophy of the search for truth, we recognize that understanding God is a never-ending journey. Each new discovery is just a starting point for a new inquiry. Each answer found raises new questions. It is in this incessant search that we find our true intellectual freedom.

In Deism, truth is not a prison, but the wings that allow us to fly higher, explore more deeply and understand the universe and our place in it more fully. It is a quest that challenges us, inspires us and enriches us as human beings.

In Deism, our intellectual freedom is the key that opens the door to the unknown and invites us to explore the infinite horizons of God's understanding. Each step on this journey is a celebration of the human mind, an ode to the ability to question, reason and discover. We are free, not to turn away from God, but to approach Him with a curious eye and an open mind. Our search for truth is the path that leads us to the heart of the universe. Thus, in Deism, we find the freedom that elevates us, enriches us and connects us to the divine in a unique and profound way.

Chapter 11
The Continuous Search for Divine Truth

We believe that the search for divine truth is a continuous journey, sustained by fundamental principles. We begin with the primacy of reason. Reason endows us with the innate ability to discern, allowing us to analyze and question the mysteries of the universe in a logical and coherent way. God gave us the ability to reason, and He wants us to use it.

With reason, intellectual freedom is another essential principle. We deeply encourage questioning, because we understand that it is the basis of intellectual progress. Questioning allows us to unveil the veils that hide divine truth under dogmas that impose a ready-made understanding which, in our view, leads us away from God rather than towards him. The freedom to question, to challenge conventions and to explore the mysteries of existence is what drives us.

While many religions insist on literalist interpretations of their sacred texts, in Deism, we use reason as a guide to examine these texts critically and contextually. We recognize that the Scriptures can contain symbolic and allegorical meanings, and reason helps us to discern these deeper meanings. Therefore, we do not accept dogma without question, but instead seek divine truth through critical exploration of these sources.

These principles, reason, intellectual freedom and the critical approach, are pillars that underpin our philosophy of life, enabling us to explore and understand God in a way that is deeply rooted in reason and the relentless pursuit of divine knowledge. With these principles firmly established, our journey progresses towards a continuous understanding of God.

As mentioned earlier, we can observe the evolution of deistic thought, demonstrating that the search for divine truth is not a static process, but a journey of growth and deepening understanding of who God really is. Reason plays a central role in this evolution.

Reason allows us to question established religious concepts and dogmas, critically evaluate religious beliefs and teachings, as well as examine Scripture and religious traditions critically and contextually. Through reason, we begin to plumb the depths of existence and question the meaning of life. Therefore, it is reason that drives the evolution of deistic thought, the same reason that brought Homo sapiens out of the caves.

Throughout history, deists have played a fundamental role in the evolution of thought. Many deist philosophers, thinkers and religious leaders have contributed to the development and promotion of deism as a philosophy that values reason, intellectual freedom and the search for truth. Their works and ideas have enriched and deepened the understanding of God in the context of our philosophy.

The evolution of deist thought is also evidenced by the recognition of the importance of diversity of religious perspectives and the search for tolerance. As human beings, we have a diversity of conceptions. Some people have a ready-made faith and accept the dogmas outlined by other people's interpretations, but deists are those who cannot conceive that the God they believe in has placed them before issues that reason, understood as the ability to understand, cannot conceive.

In this sense, deism stands out in the broad spectrum of spiritual beliefs as a rational and individualistic philosophy. It offers each person the opportunity to approach the question of God with freedom of thought and a deep appreciation for the diversity of perspectives. For deists, spirituality is a personal journey in which reason and introspection are essential tools. We recognize the existence of God, the creator of the universe, but we don't accept the idea of His direct intervention in everyday life. Instead, we seek to understand God through reflective study, dialog and exploration of beliefs. Knowledge is acquired through reflective study and personal effort; all advances in science have their roots in study. It is through study that you are reading this book now; previous study was necessary for you to understand the graphic representation of the letters. Without study, the words in this book would just be meaningless drawings. Wouldn't it be expected that understanding God would also be achieved by the same means, i.e. study rather than acceptance?

In this search for an understanding of the divine, deists engage in inter-religious dialogues, opening themselves up to the richness of different spiritual visions. They respect that each religious tradition has something to teach about God. The diversity of perspectives broadens their own vision of the divine and cultivates a deep respect for religious plurality. However, deists also preserve a fundamental principle: the spiritual quest must be sincere and disinterested. When religions are used for purposes other than bringing man and God closer together, when worldly interests are mixed with the spiritual quest, this religious conception loses credibility.

Thus, deism represents an intellectually challenging and respectful approach to religion and spirituality. It is a philosophy that celebrates the diversity of beliefs while maintaining the importance of preserving integrity in the search for divine truth. In a world full of spiritual perspectives, deists seek to balance the power of reason with the depth of the search for the divine, shaping a worldview that values freedom of thought and respect for individual choices.

Chapter 12
The Synthesis of Deistic Reason

When exploring the essence of Deism, it is impossible not to notice the profound relationship between reason and the divine nature. As a master Deist, my journey over the years has allowed me to explore the wonders of this connection and share insights into how reason applies to understanding the nature of God.

Deism is a philosophy that embraces reason as a beacon. Unlike many religious traditions that impose rigid interpretations, here we are encouraged to use our innate ability to discern. Reason is the flame that guides us, allowing us to transcend the preconceptions of religious dogma.

My journey has taught me that reason is more than an intellectual tool. It is an ally in the quest to understand the divine nature. It invites us to question, analyze and delve into the depths of existence, including the very nature of God. Each step on this journey reveals new layers of understanding.

Reason helps us to go beyond superficial appearances and probe the essence of God. It allows us to explore the meaning of life and our connection with the divine in a logical and coherent way. As a master deist, I share this vision with the hope that others can also walk this path of self-discovery and spiritual growth.

In exploring the relationship between reason and Deism, a fundamental aspect that deserves to be highlighted is the role of this intellectual faculty as a tool for theological analysis. As a Deist teacher, it is a privilege to share how reason plays a crucial role in our ability to critically examine religious texts and see beyond words or ready-made interpretations.

In deist teaching, we understand that Scripture can contain symbolic and allegorical meanings that are often obscured by literalist interpretations. This is where reason comes into play as a light that dispels the darkness of narrow interpretation. It enables us to read between the lines, to question pre-established assumptions and to seek a deeper understanding.

My journey has led me to explore religious texts with a critical perspective, recognizing that the truth often lies deeper than the words appear. Reason helps us to unravel these layers, revealing the treasures of wisdom and meaning that may go unnoticed by those who are content with a superficial understanding.

Theological analysis in Deism is not a mere intellectual activity; it is a quest for divine knowledge that transcends the boundaries of dogma and doctrine. It is a journey of self-discovery that leads us to question, reflect and expand our understanding of God. Reason is our compass on this journey, guiding our exploration of the profound and often hidden truths in the scriptures.

In Deism, we recognize that the universe is a vast and intricate system, carefully designed by the Creator. Universal harmony is the manifestation of this divine order, and it is through reason that we can begin to decipher its mysteries. Reason allows us to contemplate the natural laws that govern the workings of the universe and to appreciate the beauty of the coherence and symmetry that we find throughout creation.

My journey has led me to contemplate universal harmony with a deep sense of awe. By observing the repeated patterns in nature, from the structure of a flower to the orbit of the planets, reason helps me to recognize that there is an underlying intelligence that guides all these phenomena. It is reason that allows me to investigate these patterns and reveal the order that resides within them.

The search for universal harmony is a journey of wonder and discovery, in which reason acts as a lantern that lights the way. As we delve deeper into understanding this harmony, we begin to glimpse the underlying unity of all things. Reason helps us to see how all the elements of the universe are interconnected, like parts of a great cosmic puzzle.

Deism embraces the idea that science and spirituality need not be separate, but complementary. Reason plays a crucial role in this understanding, allowing us to examine the natural world with scientific curiosity, while at the same time exploring the spiritual dimensions of existence.

Reason has guided me along a path that values observable evidence in the natural world and scientific research as a means of understanding how God works through natural laws. Science, in the light of reason, is not seen as a threat to spirituality, but as a tool that allows us to unravel the mysteries of divine creation.

It is reason that helps us to appreciate the beauty of the harmony between science and spirituality. Rather than seeing these two perspectives as conflicting, we are encouraged to see them as parts of a greater whole. Reason allows us to integrate our scientific understanding of the world with our spiritual search for the divine.

Chapter 13
Science as an Ally in the Search for the Divine

The complex relationship between science and spirituality often raises the question of whether these approaches are conflicting or complementary. It is important to note that science and spirituality address different aspects of human existence. Science is dedicated to investigating the "how" of things, seeking to understand natural processes and the laws that govern the universe. Spirituality, on the other hand, focuses on the "why" and deeper meaning of existence, exploring questions related to morality, purpose and transcendence.

A harmonious approach between science and spirituality involves accepting that these two perspectives can coexist and even enrich each other. Many scientists and thinkers have found a source of spirituality in scientific research. By observing the complexity and order of the universe, they are inspired to explore deeper questions about existence and the divine nature.

Astronomy and astrophysics are scientific fields that often lead people to contemplate the universe with awe and reverence. By exploring the vastness of space and the wonders of the universe, science offers a window into the grandeur of creation. Often, this scientific exploration broadens the understanding of God, raising questions about the divine role in the formation of the universe.

There are areas where science and spirituality converge in their explorations. For example, the Big Bang theory, widely accepted in cosmology, describes the origin of the universe from a state of high density and temperature. Some see this cosmic event as the manifestation of God's will to create the universe. In addition, the complexity of life on Earth and the theory of evolution also raise questions about how life fits into the divine plan.

Science can be seen as a valuable tool in the spiritual journey. The search for scientific knowledge not only enriches understanding of the natural world, but also strengthens faith by revealing the beauty and harmony of the laws of nature. Many believe that the search for divine truth can be enriched by a deeper understanding of the cosmos and the mysteries of existence unraveled by science.

The scientific exploration of the universe, especially in the fields of astronomy and astrophysics, has been a constant quest to understand the secrets of the universe. This exploration offers valuable insights into the nature of the cosmos, its origins and its complexity. These insights, in turn, have a significant impact on how we perceive the divine and can enrich our spiritual journey.

Astronomy allows us to contemplate the vastness of space, with billions of galaxies, stars and planets. This cosmic immensity often evokes a sense of wonder and awe. Many consider these scientific discoveries to be the manifestation of God's greatness, questioning how such a vast and complex universe could have come into being.

In the spiritual journey, stars and planets often play a symbolic role. They are seen as reference points in the night sky, guiding people in their search for meaning. Astronomical science, by revealing the nature and formation of these celestial bodies, broadens the understanding of how the cosmos plays a role in spiritual beliefs and practices.

One of the philosophical aspects that astronomical science can corroborate is the origin of the universe from a great explosion, the so-called "Big Bang". This gigantic event generated the primordial elements which, at first, only formed cosmic dust. This dust gradually grouped together and formed molecules of other elements that would later give rise to everything we know. In this context, it can be said that you are part of the universe, because everything that makes it up was already present in the first cosmic dust. In a poetic way, I can say that you have always existed and will always exist.

Astrophysics explores the evolution of the universe, from the Big Bang to the formation of galaxies, stars and planets. This scientific account of the history of the universe raises questions about how the divine plan might be related to the expansion and development of the universe. Many see science as a way of deciphering the mysteries of divine creation.

Scientific exploration of the cosmos not only increases our understanding of the universe, but also enriches the spiritual journey. Through scientific knowledge, we can appreciate even more the complexity and beauty of divine creation. Space exploration reminds us of the vastness of the cosmos and the smallness of the Earth, which can inspire a sense of humility and reverence towards the divine.

Science is known for its rigorous scientific method, which is based on observation, experimentation, critical analysis and the formulation of testable hypotheses. This approach, centered on empirical evidence, can be adapted to investigate spiritual and religious issues, promoting a more grounded and informed search for divine knowledge.

The scientific method encourages a critical approach to evaluating and examining religious beliefs.

This does not necessarily imply discrediting such beliefs, but rather subjecting them to rational and empirical scrutiny. Through critical analysis, we can better understand the basis of religious beliefs and how they relate to our search for God.

Spirituality often deals with personal and transcendental experiences. The application of the scientific method helps us to examine these experiences from an empirical perspective. Scientific research into spiritual experiences, meditation, prayer and altered states of consciousness provides a more solid understanding of how these practices affect the connection with God.

The scientific method also encourages us to formulate testable hypotheses related to spirituality and the search for divine knowledge. This means that we can develop questions and theories that can be investigated empirically, allowing for a more systematic and directed search for divine truth.

The application of the scientific method in the search for divine knowledge does not necessarily mean conflict between science and religion. On the contrary, it can pave the way for a more harmonious integration between the two perspectives. Science can provide valuable insights that complement spiritual beliefs, creating a more holistic approach to understanding God.

One of the most significant challenges in integrating science and spirituality is the apparent conflict between religious beliefs and scientific findings. In some cases, literal interpretations of religious texts can come into direct conflict with established scientific knowledge. For example, the theory of evolution can be seen as challenging some creationist interpretations of monotheistic religions. These conflicts can create dilemmas for those seeking a broader understanding of God.

What has been built up over the ages by religious systems has created a barrier, while at the same time accommodating religious dogma so deeply in the collective subconscious that even though it cannot refute science, issues such as the evolution of the species or the Big Bang are viewed with skepticism by the most fervent religious.

To overcome the challenges in integrating science and spirituality, it is essential to adopt an approach that values both perspectives. This involves recognizing that science and spirituality are distinct domains, each with its own scope and methods. Science seeks to explain the "how" of the universe, while spirituality deals with the "why" and deeper meaning of existence.

One approach that many adopt to reconcile religious beliefs with science is the non-literal interpretation of religious texts. Instead of considering these texts as literal descriptions of events, they can be seen as allegorical or symbolic. This allows people to maintain their spiritual beliefs while accepting scientific discoveries.

In this context, we can affirm that not all the water contained in the oceans, or even in suspension, would be enough to flood the entire planet, as quoted in some scriptures. The scientific impossibility of the event known as the flood makes it necessary to accept that its description is only allegorical. This is a crucial point, after all, not accepting the description as an allegorical quotation would imply that the affirmation of the occurrence of the flood, according to science, would not correspond to the truth and this would put the rest of the content of the book where the text is inserted in doubt.

In this way, the flexible approach allows both science and spirituality to coexist in a more harmonious way, recognizing that each plays a distinct role in the search for knowledge of God. This not only enriches the understanding of the divine, but also helps to overcome the challenges and dilemmas that arise from integrating these two seemingly divergent perspectives.

Another way of integrating science and spirituality is through the application of spiritual and ethical values in the scientific context. This involves using spiritual principles, such as compassion, empathy and care for others, as guidelines for scientific research and the responsible use of technology. Integrating spiritual values can enrich scientific practice and help direct technological advances in an ethical manner.

Integrating science and spirituality also requires a willingness to embrace complexity. Not all questions have simple answers, and many aspects of the divine can remain mysterious. The search for divine knowledge is an ongoing journey, and a willingness to explore the intersections between science and spirituality can lead to a richer and more enriching understanding of the universe and God.

Chapter 14
The Deist View of God

In my quest for divine understanding, the conception of God assumes a central and transcendental role. In order to understand deism, it is vital to grasp my unique view of God.

From my perspective, God manifests himself as an immaterial entity, devoid of physical form. This conception contrasts with many religions, which personify deities as anthropomorphic beings. For me, God represents a spiritual presence that permeates the universe, simultaneously the primordial source of all things and the essence that transcends all forms. This immaterial vision of God invites me to establish a unique bond with divinity, devoid of rituals and dogmas, while seeking a more personal understanding.

In addition to his immaterial nature, I conceive of God as a transcendental entity. This implies that God is beyond comprehension, unreachable by human concepts. God's transcendence is what makes possible the existence of the universe and the natural order that regulates it. God, the supreme architect, established the laws of the universe and allowed life to flourish according to these laws, without directly interfering in human affairs.

God invites me to contemplate the mystery of existence and to seek divine understanding through reason and observation of the world around me. The search for knowledge of God, for me, represents a personal and continuous journey, an intellectual and spiritual exploration that challenges the mind and nourishes the soul. In the process, I strive to understand the purpose of life and the connection between human existence and the divine plan.

To understand the deist perspective on God, it is essential to unravel the anthropomorphic representations that often dominate traditional religious conceptions. By rejecting the notion of a God with human form, or any other way that religions portray Him, I question the limitations of the human mind and encourage everyone to transcend the common images associated with divinity.

Many religions often portray God with human characteristics, such as a face, arms, legs and emotional attributes. This anthropomorphization of God makes Him more accessible to people, allowing them to relate to a divine figure who seems understandable and close. However, I argue that this approach restricts the divine nature and imprisons God in a limited box.

In this context, it is crucial to clarify that any human attempt to represent the image of God in a plastic way is inadequate for even the most modest minds. The human form is a biological adaptation that proved necessary for the survival of the species, which over time has been refined to suit needs. It is incomprehensible that the human mind, which is rational, can conceive of a being that has not undergone these biological adaptations having a similar form.

My vision of God is of an entity so vast and complex that the human mind cannot fully grasp it. By rejecting anthropomorphic representations, I invite everyone to look beyond conventional images of God and explore the true nature of divinity. I emphasize that understanding God must be based on reason, observation of the natural order and the continuous search for knowledge. This search for the true nature of God represents an intellectual and spiritual journey that challenges the mind and expands the horizons of human understanding.

Today, I perceive the universe as a manifestation of the divine will of an immaterial and transcendental God. Instead of God being an active figure who constantly intervenes in creation, He is the creator who established the natural laws that govern the cosmos. When I adopted this perspective, I experienced profound relief, as I was freed from the image of a punitive and insensitive God who favors only a few.

My vision of God's immaterial and transcendental nature highlights the simplicity and universality of divinity. Instead of embracing complex mythologies or religious dogmas, I find beauty in the simplicity of my vision of God as the primordial cause of all that exists. This inspires me to appreciate creation in its purest form, recognizing God's presence in the harmony of the natural world.

My understanding of God's immaterial and transcendental nature also serves as a call for human responsibility in preserving and caring for creation. I believe that, as rational beings, we have an ethical and moral duty to protect the environment and promote harmony in the world. Understanding divinity as transcendental reminds me that we are part of a greater order and that our connection with God is reflected in our actions.

It is fundamental to understand how this conception of God's immaterial and transcendental nature relates to human life and the spiritual journey. I believe that this unique view of divinity has profound implications for understanding the soul, human existence and the path towards divine knowledge.

In my view, the human soul is a divine spark, a part of God's transcendental essence. This view, rooted in the immaterial nature of God, underlines the idea that each individual carries with them an intrinsic connection with the divine. The soul is perceived as immortal, not subject to physical death, and its journey is intrinsically linked to the quest for understanding God and spiritual evolution.

My belief in the search for divine knowledge is a personal and intellectual journey that involves the exploration of my own soul. I believe that by cultivating reason, ethics and contemplation, I can get closer to God. The transcendental nature of God serves as an inspiration for this continuous search, encouraging me to deepen my understanding of divinity and the universe.

I emphasize the importance of ethics as an integral part of the spiritual journey. I believe that understanding morality is intrinsically linked to understanding divine will and recognizing human responsibility in preserving balance and harmony in the world. This connection between ethics and spirituality is an essential part of my vision of the transcendental nature of God.

My understanding of God as an immaterial and transcendental entity invites contemplation. This contemplation is not restricted to specific religious rituals, but involves an intellectual and spiritual quest that invites one to meditate on the nature of the universe and its relationship with God. It is a call to deepen one's spiritual connection through reflection and the continuous search for divine knowledge.

I see the search for unity with God as the supreme goal of the spiritual journey. I believe that throughout this journey, the soul progressively draws closer to divinity, transcending the limitations of human existence and returning to unity with the transcendental. This search for unity with God represents the consummation of the spiritual journey.

However, I recognize that the search for divine knowledge and unity with God is an ongoing journey. It is not a destination, but an incessant process of spiritual improvement and reflection.

Chapter 15
The Evolution of Representations of God

Since the dawn of civilization, humanity has sought to understand the divine. In different cultures and times, we see the emergence of gods and goddesses, each reflecting the concerns, fears and aspirations of the societies that worshipped them. These divine representations were shaped according to the cultural, social and psychological needs of the time.

Deists, like myself, believe that God is a transcendental entity, a force that is beyond the capacity of the human mind to fully comprehend. However, throughout history, we have witnessed a remarkable trend: the creation of anthropomorphic representations of God. This raises an intriguing question: how can a divine and eternal being be described in such a variable and sometimes contradictory way?

In this context, we witness the creation of gods and goddesses that reflected not only the desires of ancient civilizations, but also the natural elements and cosmic forces that shaped their lives, as well as largely meeting the needs of mass control through faith.

On the banks of the Nile, the Egyptians worshipped a panoply of deities, each representing specific aspects of life, death and the afterlife. The Egyptian gods, such as Isis, Osiris and Ra, personified elements of nature and cosmic phenomena. They provided a sense of order and meaning to an often mysterious and unforgiving world.

In Ancient Greece, deities ruled Mount Olympus, each bringing a unique dimension to the human experience. Zeus, the all-powerful, symbolized authority and lightning; Aphrodite personified love and beauty; Athena represented wisdom and strategy. These gods and goddesses were anthropomorphic entities, often influenced by human passions and weaknesses.

In Ancient India, deities such as Brahma, Vishnu and Shiva personified the aspects of the cycle of life, death and rebirth. These gods were worshipped in different forms and manifestations, reflecting the spiritual complexity of Indian culture.

In China, Taoism and Confucianism shaped spiritual understanding. The Tao, an immutable cosmic force, was central to Taoism, while Confucius emphasized morality and ethics as key principles for a harmonious society.

In Rome, the gods were adapted from Greek mythology, but with different names. Jupiter, corresponding to Zeus, was the lord of the gods, while

Mars personified war and Venus, love and fertility. These divine representations played a fundamental role in Roman culture and were reflected in religion, politics and everyday life.

What makes the history of Rome even more fascinating is the religious transition that took place from 312 AD onwards. In that year, the Roman Empire faced religious and political divisions. According to historical accounts, Emperor Constantine had a remarkable vision. He reported seeing a cross in the sky with the inscription "In hoc signo vinces" (In this sign, you will win). Constantine interpreted this as a divine sign and decided to adopt the Christian symbol, known as the Chi-Rho, on the insignia of his army before battle. Surprisingly, Constantine won this decisive battle and attributed his victory to the Christian God.

The following year, in 313 AD, Constantine issued the Edict of Milan, together with the co-emperor Licinius. This is an important milestone in history, as it granted religious tolerance to all religions within the Roman Empire, including Christianity. This action encouraged religious freedom and allowed Christianity to develop without persecution.

The Christianization of the Roman Empire represented a significant religious transformation, but it also raised concerns about the fusion of the church with political power. As the Christian faith grew, the ecclesiastical institution began to acquire political influence and authority, which could be considered a distortion of the original principles of Christianity, which emphasized simplicity and morality. This also resulted in periods of religious intolerance, such as the Inquisition, which repressed any form of religious dissent, marking a challenging period in the history of Christianity.

The Middle Ages was a period marked by significant changes in religious views and understanding of God. During the Middle Ages, the influence of Christianity spread throughout Europe and beyond, profoundly shaping the conception of God for many. In this context, the view of God became increasingly influenced by the scriptures and teachings of the Bible.

The Abrahamic God, worshipped by Judaism, Christianity and Islam, emerged as the central figure. This God was often represented as the creator of the universe, the supreme judge and ruler of all creation. He was perceived as a being who actively intervenes in human life, guiding destinies, distributing rewards and punishments and electing for himself a few chosen ones.

The Christian churches of the Middle Ages emphasized the authority of the clergy and the need for religious mediation to achieve salvation. The Catholic Church played a dominant role in people's lives, controlling not only spiritual aspects, but also political and social ones. God was often represented as a distant figure, whose access was mediated by the religious hierarchy.

However, it was also a period of intense devotion and spiritual searching. Gothic cathedrals, such as Notre-Dame Cathedral, are impressive witnesses to this devotion, with their majestic architecture and stained glass windows that tell biblical stories. During this period, people sought God through rituals, prayers and pilgrimages, seeking a direct connection with the divine. However, in my opinion, this approach can be seen as contradictory to the view of God as an omnipresent entity, since He is everywhere.

The influence of the Christian philosopher Thomas Aquinas brought a new dimension to the understanding of God. He argued that human reason could be used to better understand God and his relationship with the world. This synthesis between faith and reason had a lasting impact on Christian theology.

However, the God of the Middle Ages often became a fearsome being, associated with harsh judgments and divine punishments. The vision of a vengeful and implacable God led to widespread fear and a desperate search for redemption.

Deism emerged as a response to this vision of God. We affirm that God is a transcendental and benevolent entity, not limited by human representations or human fear. For deists, God is the creator of the universe, but also the impartial observer who allows the world to take its natural course, without arbitrary intervention.

Deism challenges us to seek a deeper understanding of God, one that goes beyond cultural representations and images of an anthropomorphic God. Our vision of God as an entity that transcends all human representations invites us to explore the divine nature in a more open and broader way.

As we explore the evolution of representations of God, let's remember that these visions are shaped by the cultural, psychological and political needs of their times. Each era brings with it its own unique understanding of God, and Deism invites us to critically reflect on these representations in search of a deeper and more universal understanding of the divine nature by questioning and challenging preconceived concepts, seeking the fullest understanding of divinity.

The Renaissance was marked by an explosion of creativity, critical thinking and a rediscovery of the importance of individuality.

In the Renaissance, the focus on understanding God took a new direction. The emphasis was on the human capacity for reason, exploration and creative expression. Artists such as Leonardo da Vinci and Michelangelo created masterpieces that captured the imagination and celebrated the beauty of human existence.

The vision of God began to move away from the authoritarian and distant representations of the Middle Ages. Renaissance philosophers explored ideas about the nature of God that emphasized the connection between the divine and the human. They argued that the search for knowledge and artistic expression were ways of getting closer to God.

The notion that the quest for knowledge was a spiritual journey gained prominence. The study of natural sciences, such as astronomy and anatomy, was seen as a way to better understand creation. This challenged traditional views of God as a supernatural entity that directly interfered in the world.

As individuality and personal expression flourished, new interpretations of God also emerged. Philosophers such as Giordano Bruno proposed ideas that questioned the conventional view of God. He argued that God was an immanent force in the universe, present in all things.

The Renaissance was a period of intellectual exploration and expansion of the frontiers of human thought. It was an era that encouraged the search for a more personal and direct understanding of God, in contrast to the impersonal and authoritarian view that prevailed in the Middle Ages.

However, as we move forward on our journey of exploration, we are reminded that representations of God continue to evolve. Each era brings its own perspectives and challenges, and our understanding of divinity continues to expand, even though the God we believe in remains the same.

Chapter 16
The Evolution of Representations of God

The Scientific Revolution, which reached its apogee in the 16th and 17th centuries, shed new light on the nature of the universe and, consequently, on our understanding of God.

In the period following the Enlightenment, renowned scientists such as Galileo Galilei, Johannes Kepler and Isaac Newton led a real revolution in understanding the natural laws that govern the universe. Their discoveries, such as the laws of motion and the law of gravity, provided a more coherent and comprehensive view of how the universe works.

This new understanding raised significant questions about the relationship between God and creation. Mechanicism, a philosophical perspective that conceived of the universe as a perfectly ordered machine, led some to conceive of God as a great divine watchmaker. From this perspective, God planned the universe and set it in motion, without directly interfering in its functioning.

This representation of God as the "Divine Watchmaker" emphasized the order and regularity of the universe, reflecting the natural laws discovered by science. However, it also distanced God from the sphere of direct intervention in human life, as the search for rational and natural explanations for phenomena previously considered miraculous became more common.

For deists, this view was compatible with their belief in a God who created the universe, but who did not constantly interfere in human life. Science, in this sense, was considered a tool for unraveling the wonders of divine creation.

As science advanced, new discoveries continued to challenge traditional conceptions of God. Theories such as Charles Darwin's evolution and the Big Bang theory transformed our understanding of the origin of life and the universe. These theories offered natural explanations for phenomena that had previously been attributed to the direct action of God.

Deists faced the challenge of reconciling these new discoveries with their belief in a creator God. Many argued that science and religion were not mutually exclusive, but complementary approaches to understanding the universe. For them, science revealed how God's natural laws operated in the world, while religion continued to explore questions of meaning and purpose.

As knowledge expanded, we reached a point where the conception of God as an expression of universal mystery plays a central role in deist spirituality. This vision transcends anthropomorphic representations and invites us to contemplate divinity in a more abstract and universal way.

At the heart of this representation is the idea that God is the manifestation of the cosmic mystery that permeates the universe. This is not a distant and personal God, but an immanent presence that reveals itself in every aspect of creation. For deists, God is found in the order and harmony of the cosmos, in the beauty of nature and in the complexity of the natural world.

This vision of God as an expression of universal mystery invites us to transcend limited concepts and connect with something that is beyond comprehension. It is a call to humility, awe and reverence before the vastness of the universe and divine nature.

For deists, this spiritual perspective is deeply inspiring. It reminds us that we are part of something bigger and that our spiritual journey involves exploring this universal mystery. Every scientific discovery, every moment of wonder at nature and every deep reflection on the cosmos brings us closer to this understanding.

The expression of universal mystery also challenges us to embrace the diversity of beliefs and religions in the world. We recognize that different spiritual traditions offer varying visions of God, each capturing an aspect of the infinite. Rather than dividing, this vision unites us in our quest for divine knowledge.

Ultimately, understanding God as an expression of universal mystery invites us to embrace the beauty of uncertainty and the richness of ongoing spiritual exploration. It is a journey in which we do not seek definitive answers, but a deeper connection with the divine through contemplation of the mystery that permeates creation.

The evolution of representations of God leads us to an intriguing intersection: how the concept of God in Deism relates to traditional religious institutions and, at the same time, to individual spirituality. This is a fundamental starting point for understanding the deist perspective on the role of religions and the personal spiritual quest.

In Deism, we often find a healthy tension between the understanding of the divine as the universal mystery and the dynamics of organized religions. Deists value the diversity of religious traditions in the world, recognizing that each offers a unique lens through which to contemplate spirituality.

On the one hand, traditional religious institutions have played a significant role in human history, providing frameworks for worship, ethics and community. However, deists opt for a more personal spiritual path, preferring a direct relationship with the divine, free from dogmatic structures and ritualistic practices. In this sense, many people adopt deistic practices even without realizing it, since it is common in modern society to no longer attend church, since the concept of an omnipresent God allows contact with Him anywhere. The most common response among people who adopt this practice is: "I don't need to go to church to talk to God".

For deists, the personal search for God is a deeply meaningful act. Individual spirituality allows for a freer and more open exploration of the divine, without the restrictions of specific religious doctrines. It is a journey that encourages self-discovery, contemplation and the search for divine knowledge on a personal level.

This direct relationship with the divine also manifests itself in the way deists interpret religious texts. Instead of rigidly adhering to sacred scriptures, deists tend to use them as sources of inspiration and reflection. We look for personal meaning in the words, exploring how these scriptures relate to our understanding of God.

Deism embraces spirituality as an ongoing journey, encouraging people to constantly seek a deeper understanding of God and the universe. There is no rigid dogma that defines the deist faith; instead, faith is shaped by personal search and contemplation of the universal mystery.

This spiritual approach is a reflection of the inquisitive spirit of deists, who value reason, science and the search for truth. We believe that the search for God should not be limited by religious boundaries.

At the heart of Deism is the belief that God is a perennial source of inspiration and guidance. As we explore how representations of God have evolved throughout human history, it is crucial to understand how deists see the divine as a force that influences their lives in practical and meaningful ways.

Deists find inspiration in contemplating the grandeur and complexity of the universe. When they look at the cosmos, they see God's hand in the order and beauty of the natural world. This inspiring vision of the divine encourages us to seek a deeper understanding of nature and the mysteries of the universe.

Divine guidance also plays a crucial role in deistic spirituality. We believe that God not only created the universe, but also established laws and principles that govern how the world works. We see these laws as a guide to living an ethical and moral life.

Seeking divine guidance involves reflecting on these natural laws and applying them to life. Deists believe that by living in harmony with divine laws, they can achieve a state of balance and inner peace. This leads them to make ethical decisions and act compassionately towards others.

God is seen as a constant and beneficial presence, offering subtle guidance through observation and contemplation of the world. Nature, for deists, is an open book that reveals divine principles, and they study it with reverence.

The deist vision of God as a source of inspiration and practical guidance transcends the boundaries of organized religion. It invites each individual to find meaning and purpose in their own spiritual journey. Deists value the freedom to seek God in a personal way, while also striving to live by the ethical and moral principles they consider fundamental.

It is important to emphasize that Deism is an ongoing journey. The search for divine knowledge in Deism is never complete, as it is intrinsically linked to the search for an understanding of the complexity of the universe and human nature.

In Deism, we value reflection, questioning and the constant search for truth. We believe that understanding God and the divine is a journey that lasts a lifetime and goes beyond it. It is a journey that leads us to explore not only the cosmos and human existence, but also our own nature and purpose.

Deism does not seek simplistic answers or inflexible dogmas. Instead, it encourages critical thinking and intellectual exploration. The evolution of representations of God is a manifestation of this ongoing search for understanding. As humanity evolves, so does our vision of the divine, reflecting our intellectual and spiritual progress.

This philosophy challenges us to remain open to new discoveries and to recognize that our representations of God are only human attempts to capture the ineffable. We cannot claim to fully understand the divine mystery, but we can strive to approach it through contemplation, reflection and the constant search for knowledge.

I invite you to keep an open mind to the mysteries that Deism has to offer. In Deism, we find a path that allows us to explore our spirituality in a personal way, while also embracing the ethical and moral principles that we consider fundamental.

Chapter 17
The Universality of the Search for God

The universal search for God is a journey that transcends cultures and eras. Since the dawn of humanity, people have looked to the starry sky, to natural phenomena and to their own inner selves in search of answers about existence and the divine. This search knows no geographical boundaries, language barriers or time limits.

Deists have a deep understanding of this innate search for God, because it lies at the heart of our faith. The deist vision of God as the Creator of the universe and of natural laws resonates with the observation of the order and beauty that permeate the cosmos. The universality of this quest is a testament to the intrinsic connection between humanity and the divine.

Throughout history, different cultures have developed their own representations and concepts of God, shaped by their unique cultural contexts, experiences and understandings. However, regardless of the specific representations, the search for divine truth remains a common thread that unites all civilizations.

Deists recognize the diversity of religious beliefs and practices around the world and respect the richness of this spiritual landscape. We see this diversity as an expression of the human quest for a deeper understanding of divinity. After all, the search for God is not only an intellectual journey, but also a journey of the heart and soul.

As we explore the universality of the search for God, I invite you to reflect on the beauty of this diversity and to understand that, despite external differences, we all share an intrinsic desire to connect with something greater than ourselves. It is in this search that we find our shared humanity and the divine spark that dwells in each of us.

The universal search for God is deeply interwoven into the fabric of human religion and spirituality. Human history is full of religious traditions that offer diverse and rich interpretations of divinity. Deists recognize and respect this religious diversity as part of the human search for God.

In contrast to many religious traditions, Deism stands out for its particular approach. We see God as the Creator, but not as a being who directly interferes in human life. This view can be seen as an attempt to understand God in a more rational way, away from the anthropomorphic representations that are often found in traditional religions.

The relationship between the concept of God in Deism and traditional religious institutions can be complex. While some people find comfort and guidance in these institutions, others seek a more personal and individual spirituality. Deists value freedom of spiritual choice, believing that a connection with God can be found both inside and outside conventional religious structures.

Individual spirituality plays a fundamental role in the journey of many deists. We see God as a source of inspiration and guidance in our daily lives, even if we don't follow specific religious rituals. Divinity is a constant presence in our reflections and in the way we seek to live meaningful and ethical lives.

The universality of the search for God is reflected in the diversity of religions and belief systems that humanity embraces. In Deism, we find our own interpretation of this divine mystery, one that emphasizes human rationality and autonomy. Regardless of our spiritual approach, the search for God remains a constant in our lives, a search that connects us with something transcendental and eternal.

On our deistic journey, we realize that God is much more than an intellectual abstraction. He is a source of deep inspiration and guidance. We see God as the supreme principle of existence.

The deistic vision of God as a source of inspiration invites us to contemplate the divine in every aspect. Every sunset, every act of kindness, and every moment of admiration for the beauty of the natural world are reflections of God in our daily lives. This perception inspires us to live with gratitude and appreciation, valuing every experience as a divine gift.

In addition to inspiration, God is also a moral compass. We believe that understanding divinity guides us in our search for truth, justice and compassion. By internalizing the deistic principle, we are encouraged to make ethical decisions, to respect the dignity of all human beings and to seek the common good.

Seeing God as a guiding presence also helps us to face personal challenges. In times of difficulty, we find strength in the belief that God is with us, offering support. This faith enables us to overcome obstacles, to grow as individuals and to deal with life's adversities with courage and determination.

God is our constant inspiration and moral compass. He reminds us of the beauty of the world and guides us in our search for truth and compassion. The deist view of God as a source of inspiration and guidance not only enriches our lives, but also motivates us to seek divine wisdom in every aspect of existence.

Deistic philosophy is not just an abstract theory, but a philosophy that can be lived and practiced in everyday life. It invites us to apply deistic principles and beliefs in all areas of life, transforming our actions and perspectives.

One of the fundamental principles of Deism, as insistently emphasized, is the cultivation of reason and critical thinking. We believe that reason is a divine gift that enables us to understand the world and seek divine knowledge. In practice, this means that we constantly seek to expand our understanding, questioning dogmas and prejudices, and adopting a rational approach to problem-solving.

Ethics also plays a central role in deist philosophy. We believe that morality does not necessarily depend on specific religious beliefs, but is a universal principle that transcends these boundaries. In practice, this means that we strive to live ethical lives, based on principles such as compassion, justice and respect for others.

For example, consider two people: one who chooses not to commit theft based on fear of legal or divine consequences, and another who makes this choice guided by their ethical and moral code, which simply does not allow the act of theft. This is deistic spirituality; it is not driven by a system of rewards and punishments. We seek God because we want to find Him, not because we long for a place in paradise.

This spirituality manifests itself in the constant search for divine knowledge. We seek to understand more about the nature of God, the universe and our own existence. In practice, this leads us to explore areas such as philosophy, science, art and spirituality, seeking deep connections between these fields of study.

Another practical aspect of Deism is respect for individual freedom of belief and thought. We believe that each person has the right to follow their own spiritual journey and seek the truth according to their conscience. This translates into an inclusive and tolerant approach towards the beliefs of others.

Deistic philosophy, in practice, involves integrating deistic principles into daily life. We seek reason, ethics, spirituality and freedom of thought as ways of getting closer to God. Deism is not just a philosophy, but a practical guide to a life of reflection, compassion and the constant search for divine knowledge.

By exploring deistic philosophy, we arrive at a unique vision of God as an expression of the universal mystery. For us, God is not a distant or unattainable entity, but a manifestation of this mystery that permeates the entire cosmos.

This perspective invites us to contemplate the vastness and complexity of the universe as a direct expression of God. Every star in the sky, every tree in the forest and every human being on Earth is part of this intricate divine puzzle. God is not separate from creation; he is intrinsic to it.

In practice, this vision encourages us to develop a deep reverence for nature and all forms of life. We see the universe as a sacred temple, and every experience as an opportunity to connect with the divine. Through contemplating the beauty of nature and the wonder of the cosmos, we find spiritual inspiration.

This understanding of God as an expression of the universal mystery also leads us to a constant search for answers to the great questions of existence. We question, explore and reflect on the mysteries of life and death, of meaning and purpose. Every search for knowledge is a search for a deeper understanding of God.

Deistic spirituality is enriched by recognizing that the universal mystery is unfathomable, and that our search for God is a never-ending journey. This search is not only driven by the desire to know divinity, but also by the desire to know ourselves more deeply. As we explore the mysteries of the universe, we also explore the mysteries of our own existence.

God as an expression of the universal mystery reminds us that life is a spiritual journey, full of discoveries and reflections. Every moment, every challenge and every joy are opportunities to draw closer to God and connect with the mystery that permeates everything that exists. This is the essence of deistic spirituality in practice.

Chapter 18
Understanding God in the Modern Age

As we approach the deistic view of God in the modern age, let me take you through an in-depth analysis of how our divine understanding aligns with the contemporary understanding of the universe and human existence.

Today, science and philosophy have advanced considerably. The complexities of the universe have been revealed through astronomy and quantum physics; the origins of life have been unraveled by biology; and the nuances of the human mind have been deciphered by psychology. These scientific and philosophical triumphs do not diminish our deistic view of God, but enrich it.

We deists conceive of God as the great architect of the universe, the creator of the natural laws that govern the entire cosmos. As we unravel these laws through science, we are in fact unraveling God's plans. Each scientific discovery presents itself as a revelation of God's knowledge, giving us the opportunity to admire the complexity and order that permeate the universe.

The deist understanding of God also harmonizes with the modern understanding of human existence. Here, we recognize human autonomy and responsibility in shaping our destiny. We are not mere spectators of life, but co-authors of our own journey. Freedom of thought and the ability to make ethical decisions are divine gifts that enable us to forge our own path.

In this constantly evolving scenario, the deistic vision invites us to adopt a rational and compassionate approach. We foster respect for diversity of thought and belief, value individual freedom and seek knowledge and truth in a world flooded with information.

Understanding God in the modern age teaches us that spirituality is a dynamic journey, not a static one. We continue to seek a deeper understanding of God and the universe, keeping our minds open to future discoveries. This openness helps us to grow both as individuals and as a society, in a constant dialog between faith and reason.

In Deism, understanding God is not a barrier to progress, but a source of inspiration for exploring the mysteries of the universe. We see science and spirituality as complementary. Both have the potential to uplift us and guide us in the search for truth, whether that truth is revealed through observation of the cosmos or contemplation of the divine.

Thus, in the modern age, our deistic vision of God remains alive and relevant as we seek to unite the wonders of science and spirituality in our journey towards divine knowledge.

Our faith teaches us that God transcends our understanding. His greatness and complexity are truly infinite.

This universal mystery inspires us to contemplate the cosmos and existence with a sense of awe and reverence. Every aspect of the universe, from the vastness of galaxies to the complexity of subatomic particles, is seen as part of God's great plan. Everything is interconnected in a cosmic dance of energy and matter, reflecting divine wisdom.

In our search for God, we are inspired to explore the secrets of nature, to unravel the enigmas of space and to investigate the mysteries of the human mind. Each discovery, each scientific revelation, brings us closer to understanding that God is present in every aspect of life.

We understand that God is not just a distant, abstract figure, but an immanent presence in all that is. God is in the winds that blow, the trees that grow, the rivers that flow and the stars that shine in the night sky.

God is the fabric that binds all creation together, the breath that gives life.

This vision leads us to a deep spiritual connection with the natural world, valuing nature as the tangible manifestation of God. Our spirituality is rooted in reverence for creation and the desire to care for and preserve the world that God has given us.

As we contemplate the universal mystery, our faith teaches us that the search for God is an infinite journey. Each revelation, no matter how profound, opens doors to new questions and challenges. We are humble before the divine mystery and recognize that our understanding will never be complete.

In Deism, we find inspiration in the universal mystery, the relentless pursuit of knowledge and reverence for the wonder of existence. Our faith motivates us to explore the limits of human knowledge, while recognizing that, in the end, the greatest mystery of all is the nature of God.

It is crucial to consider how the deistic view of God aligns with the modern understanding of the universe and human existence, ever since deism was conceived.

In the modern era, we have witnessed incredible advances in science and philosophy. Extraordinary discoveries in the fields of astronomy, physics, biology and neuroscience have broadened our understanding of the universe and of ourselves. At first glance, it might seem that these discoveries challenge belief in a creator God. However, deists see harmony between science and spirituality.

Modern science, with its complex theories and technological advances, allows us to explore the cosmos on scales that were previously unimaginable. Our telescopes map distant galaxies, and particle accelerators reveal the secrets of the subatomic universe. These discoveries don't diminish our faith, they enrich it.

For deists, the universe is the great book of God's creation, and science is the tool that allows us to read it. Each new scientific discovery is seen as a revelation of the divine plan. The more we understand how the universe works, the more we admire the greatness of the mind that conceived it.

The deist view of God as the architect of the universe aligns well with the Big Bang theory, for example. We see the moment of creation as the instant when God established the natural laws that govern the cosmos, allowing the universe to evolve and expand over time. Darwin's theory of evolution is also seen as part of the divine plan, a process by which life developed and adapted to its environment.

In addition, modern neuroscience teaches us about the complexity of the human brain, the seat of our consciousness and thought. Deists see the human mind as a manifestation of the divine spark that dwells in everyone. The ability to question, reflect and seek the truth is seen as God's gift, which allows us to seek divine knowledge.

In the modern age, our understanding of God expands as we integrate scientific advances with our spirituality. The divine mystery does not diminish with the progress of science, but becomes deeper and more complex. We believe that as we explore the cosmos and the human mind, we come closer and closer to understanding God as the great architect and creator of all that exists.

In Deism, we understand that God is intrinsically linked to the unfathomable mystery that permeates the universe. The universal mystery is the essence of everything that exists, and God is the manifestation of this mystery in our human understanding. It's like contemplating the vastness of the ocean and recognizing a single drop as an integral part of it.

The deist view of God as an expression of the universal mystery invites us to embrace humility in the face of the grandeur of the cosmos. We recognize that, despite all the scientific and philosophical advances, there are limits to our understanding. We are like children in front of a vast horizon of knowledge, just beginning to unravel its secrets.

This humility in the face of universal mystery inspires us to seek a deeper connection with God through contemplation and reflection. Deists see meditation and introspection as powerful tools for connecting with the divine. By silencing our minds and opening our hearts, we can feel God's presence more intensely.

Deistic spirituality is enriched by the realization that, even as we explore the mystery of the cosmos and the human mind, there are aspects of the divine that will remain unfathomable. This reminds us that the search for God is an ongoing journey, never fully completed. Each answer reveals new questions, and each discovery leads us to explore further.

The deist view of God as an expression of universal mystery also teaches us to appreciate the beauty and complexity of creation. Every aspect of nature, from the majesty of a mountain to the delicacy of a flower, is seen as a manifestation of the divine. God is present in all things, and our task is to recognize Him in the wonder of the world around us.

So, as we explore the conception of God as an expression of the universal mystery, we are invited to embrace humility, contemplation and appreciation of creation. We see spirituality as a journey that takes us deeper into mystery, always seeking a deeper understanding of the divine.

It is essential to emphasize that the search for divine knowledge is a continuous journey, full of reflections and discoveries. Deism is not a static faith, but a philosophy that encourages us to constantly explore the relationship between humanity and God.

Deism is a philosophy that celebrates freedom of thought and the search for truth. It is not a faith that demands conformity, rigid dogmas or fixed beliefs. Instead, it is a call to explore, question and reflect. It is a journey that challenges us to grow spiritually and become more compassionate and aware people.

Our journey in Deism is like a walk along an endless road. As we advance, we encounter diverse landscapes, unexpected challenges and rewarding surprises. Each step is an opportunity for learning and growth.

Chapter 19
Humanity and the Search for God

As we contemplate the nature of the search for God and the journey of Deism, it is important to highlight the underlying unity of all humanity in this endeavor. Regardless of our origin, culture or individual beliefs, the search for the divine is a constant that connects us as human beings.

Our ancestors from different cultures and times sought to understand the transcendental, expressing it in a variety of ways. The religions and philosophies that have emerged throughout history were attempts to capture and understand divinity, reflecting the innate search for connection with something greater than ourselves.

Deism, with its emphasis on reason, freedom of thought and the search for truth, fits harmoniously into this universal tapestry. It is a manifestation of the human quest to understand the divine, a quest that transcends geographical and temporal boundaries.

In this sense, Deism reminds us that although we may have different approaches to spirituality, we all share the same aspiration for a deeper understanding of the cosmos and humanity's role in it. We are all pilgrims on the journey of knowledge.

As we face our differences and embrace our unity in the search for God, we find common ground that unites us as human beings. This shared understanding invites us to embrace the diversity of perspectives and celebrate the beauty of the spiritual quest in all its forms.

Therefore, Deism reminds us not only of the importance of the personal search for truth, but also of our connection to all of humanity in this eternal quest. May we continue our spiritual journey with humility, compassion and a deep respect for others, recognizing that we all share the desire to reach the divine.

In the relationship between deism and the search for God, it is fundamental to consider the religious diversity that permeates our society. We live in a world rich in spiritual traditions, each with its own unique vision of God. Deism invites us to embrace this diversity and to seek reconciliation between different religious beliefs.

Respect for the plurality of beliefs is essential to promote understanding and harmony between people. Deism teaches us that, although we may have different perspectives on God, we all share the goal of understanding something greater. This common understanding can unite us in a spirit of cooperation and mutual respect.

Reconciliation with religious diversity also implies recognizing that no individual view of God is absolute. Each spiritual tradition has its own valuable truths and insights, and we can learn a lot from exploring these differences. Rather than seeing diversity as an obstacle, Deism encourages us to see it as an opportunity for spiritual enrichment.

In this way, we can work together to build a world where religious freedom is respected and where people of all faiths can coexist peacefully. As we move forward on the journey of the search for God, we must remember that although we may walk different paths, we are all united in the search for spiritual truth and connection with the divine.

In exploring the relationship between Deism and the search for God, it is crucial to consider the ongoing dialog between science and spirituality. In modern times, science has played a significant role in understanding the universe and human existence. Deism invites us to embrace this dialog and explore how science and spirituality can coexist harmoniously.

For deists, science and spirituality are not mutually exclusive; on the contrary, they are complementary. Science offers us a window to understand the natural laws that govern the cosmos, while spirituality invites us to explore deeper questions about the meaning of existence and our connection with God.

The scientific method, with its emphasis on observation, experimentation and logical analysis, provides us with a solid basis for exploring the material world. At the same time, spirituality invites us to explore the inner world of consciousness, morality and transcendence.

The modern understanding of the cosmos, with its surprising discoveries about the nature of the universe, need not be seen as a threat to deistic faith. Instead, we can see it as an opportunity to marvel at the complexity and beauty of creation. Science helps us understand how the universe operates, while spirituality helps us assign meaning to that operation.

Our search for God need not ignore scientific advances; on the contrary, it is enriched by them. The deist view of God as the architect of the universe aligns with many scientific principles that describe the cosmos as an interconnected creation governed by natural laws.

We therefore invite scientists to explore the depths of spirituality and spiritual seekers to embrace scientific knowledge with curiosity and wonder. Deism reminds us that the search for God and the quest to understand the natural world can coexist, forming an enriching journey that brings us closer to a deeper understanding of the universe and our connection with the divine.

For deists, the belief in a God who does not directly interfere in human affairs does not diminish the importance of spirituality and connection with the divine in our daily lives.

God is often seen as a source of inspiration for the search for truth, knowledge and personal improvement. The deistic vision of a God who established natural laws and allowed humanity to discover them through reason encourages us to explore the world with an open and curious mind. This inspires us to seek answers to the mysteries of the cosmos and to better understand the purpose of our existence.

Divine guidance also plays a fundamental role in the life of a deist. Although we believe that God does not intervene directly in our lives, the vision of a God who has established a divine order in the universe encourages us to act ethically and morally. Seeking divine guidance helps us make thoughtful decisions, act with compassion and live according to high principles.

In addition, God serves as a source of comfort and hope in times of challenge and adversity. Deistic spirituality teaches us to trust in divine wisdom and to find meaning even in the most difficult situations. God is the lighthouse that guides us through the storms of life, offering consolation and inner strength.

In our continuous journey in search of God, we understand that His inspiration and guidance are treasures that enrich our lives. We see spirituality as a path that helps us grow as a person and contribute to a better world. When we are inspired by God and guided by high principles, we are better prepared to face the challenges of human existence with dignity and compassion.

As a deist teacher, it is my duty to explain how the principles and beliefs we discussed earlier can be translated into actions and attitudes that shape our lives.

Deistic philosophy in practice emphasizes the importance of constantly seeking divine knowledge and applying this knowledge to our earthly existence. Deism encourages us to cultivate an open and inquisitive mind, to question established beliefs and to explore the mysteries of the universe.

For a deist, the practice of deism involves the active search for truth, the understanding of divine nature and the enhancement of one's connection with God. This can be achieved through reflection, meditation and the pursuit of knowledge in various forms, such as science, philosophy and art.

Ethics and morality play a central role in deistic philosophy in practice. We believe that acting ethically and compassionately is a direct expression of our connection with God. Therefore, we strive to live according to high principles, treating others with respect, compassion and justice.

The deist philosophy also leads us to recognize the importance of freedom of thought and belief. We value individual autonomy and respect different forms of spirituality and belief. We believe that each person has the right to seek their own understanding of God and the universe, as long as this is done with integrity and respect for others.

In practicing Deism, we seek to live a balanced life, where spirituality and reason coexist harmoniously. We value earthly life as a precious opportunity for spiritual growth and self-knowledge. We see every challenge as a learning opportunity and every moment of joy as a divine gift.

Therefore, deistic philosophy in practice is an invitation to live a fulfilling life, guided by the search for truth, ethics and the connection with the divine. It is a journey of self-discovery and spiritual growth that helps us give meaning to existence and contribute to a more compassionate and harmonious world.

Chapter 20
God as an Expression of the Universal Mystery

So far, I have tried to point us in the direction that leads to a deep understanding of how Deism relates to the universal search for God and how we apply this philosophy in our daily lives. Now, we delve into the depths of the universal mystery and explore how God is perceived as its ultimate expression.

For us deists, God is seen as the supreme manifestation of this mystery that permeates the entire universe. We see the universe as an unfathomable wonder, full of order and beauty, reflecting the intelligence of the Creator. Every scientific discovery, every careful observation of nature, leads us to a deep sense of reverence for the cosmic mystery.

The vision of God as the expression of universal mystery inspires us to explore, question and seek knowledge incessantly. We recognize that our understanding of God and the universe is limited, but this limitation does not stop us from continuing the search. On the contrary, it motivates us to persevere in exploring this infinite mystery.

Deistic spirituality is deeply influenced by this perception of God as the universal mystery. Our connection with the divine is not limited to rituals or dogmas, but is a continuous quest to unravel the secrets of the cosmos and understand our own existence within this context.

Contemplating this mystery leads us to a deep sense of humility and wonder. We recognize that we are part of something much bigger than ourselves and that our existence is a tiny fragment of this cosmic mystery. This humility encourages us to act with compassion and responsibility towards the planet and all the life forms that inhabit it.

Therefore, the vision of God as the expression of the universal mystery is a cornerstone of deist spirituality. It connects us with the grandeur of the universe and inspires us to seek truth and understanding, while living with gratitude and respect for the mystery that surrounds us.

As we move forward in our exploration of Deism and the vision of God as the expression of universal mystery, it is crucial to consider how this understanding aligns with the modern age and advances in the understanding of the universe and human existence.

In the modern era, we have witnessed extraordinary advances in science, cosmology and philosophy. Our understanding of the universe has expanded exponentially, and many of the old conceptions about the cosmos have been revised in the light of new scientific evidence and theories.

For us deists, this expansion of knowledge is not seen as a threat to spirituality, but as an opportunity to deepen our understanding of God. We see science as a powerful tool for exploring the mystery of the universe, which we consider to be a manifestation of divinity.

The Big Bang theory, for example, does not contradict the view of God as the creator of the universe, but deepens our appreciation for the majesty of this creative act. We see evolution as a process that reveals the complexity and diversity of life, without denying the possibility of an intelligence behind this process.

Our understanding of God in the modern age is shaped by the wonder we feel when we contemplate the vastness of space, the fundamental laws of physics and the intricate web of life on Earth. While many traditional religious beliefs struggle to reconcile their dogmas with modern science, we deists embrace this convergence as an opportunity for spiritual growth.

The vision of God as the expression of universal mystery leads us to a deeper appreciation of the complexity and interconnectedness of all things. We see the universe as a constantly evolving work of art, and our scientific understanding is only one way of unlocking its secrets.

Therefore, in the modern age, our understanding of God expands as our understanding of the universe deepens. The deistic vision invites us to embrace the search for divine knowledge as a continuous journey, where science and spirituality are not in conflict, but complement each other.

Our search for God in the modern age is illuminated by the light of reason and the brilliance of the stars. We continue to explore the universal mystery, while embracing scientific and philosophical advances as stepping stones on our spiritual journey. Understanding God is an endless quest, one that uplifts us, inspires us and connects us with the cosmos and with our own divine essence.

Continuing on our journey of understanding Deism and the vision of God as the expression of universal mystery, it is essential to explore more deeply how this conception influences Deist spirituality.

For us deists, the idea that God is the manifestation of this cosmic mystery elevates our spirituality to a higher level of contemplation and wonder. When we contemplate the cosmos, the natural laws that govern it and the intricate web of life on Earth, we see the reflection of the divine in everything.

This vision inspires a deep sense of reverence for creation and the universe as a whole. It is a call to silent contemplation, to admire the wonders of existence and to constantly seek to understand the complexities of the world.

Deistic spirituality is not limited to rigid rituals or dogmas; it manifests itself in the continuous search for personal connection with the universal mystery. Instead of adhering to prescribed religious practices, we deists are encouraged to explore the divine through observation of nature, philosophical reflection and the search for knowledge.

This flexible and open spiritual approach allows each person to find their own way to connect with God. Some may seek inspiration in contemplating the stars, while others may find God in the beauty of art or the depth of philosophy. Deistic spirituality is a personal and unique quest that honors the diversity of human experiences.

Moreover, this vision of God as the expression of universal mystery leads us to a deep respect for the interconnectedness of all forms of life. We recognize that we are part of a greater whole, that all creatures share the same divine origin and that we are all guardians of the Earth.

Therefore, deist spirituality also manifests itself in a deep commitment to ethics and environmental responsibility. We see the preservation of the environment as a practical expression of our devotion to the divine, caring for the creation entrusted to us.

The vision of God as the expression of the universal mystery enriches deist spirituality. It invites us to contemplate the beauty and complexity of the universe, to seek God in our individual experiences and to act responsibly towards the natural world. This spirituality is a continuous journey of reflection and discovery that connects us more deeply with the mystery that permeates all existence.

In exploring the deist view of God as the expression of universal mystery, it is natural for questions to arise about the relationship between this perspective and traditional religious institutions, as well as individual spirituality.

We Deists recognize that, throughout history, humanity has developed various religions and spiritual beliefs, each with its own interpretation of God and its own specific rituals. However, Deism is distinguished by its freer approach and its detachment from conventional religious structures.

For us, God is perceived as the creator of the universe and the natural laws that govern it, not as a deity who directly interferes in human life or demands ritual devotions. This view may raise questions about the relationship between Deism and organized religions.

Importantly, many Deists respect the religious beliefs of others and recognize the value of religious institutions in providing moral guidance, community support and a space for spiritual expression. However, they choose to follow a more independent spiritual path, based on reason, observation of nature and a personal search for the divine.

This spiritual independence does not prevent deists from engaging in constructive dialogues with those who have different religious beliefs. They can share perspectives on ethical and moral issues, contributing to a more compassionate and tolerant world.

In addition, deist spirituality encourages individual reflection and the development of personal morality. We deists believe that a direct connection with God through the contemplation of nature and the search for knowledge can inspire ethics based on understanding and respect.

The deist view of God goes beyond mere intellectual contemplation. For us, God is a constant source of inspiration and guidance. Understanding a God who established natural laws and allowed human reason to discover them has profound implications for our personal journey.

We see God as the essence of knowledge and wisdom. The search for divine knowledge is not only an intellectual activity, but also a spiritual journey. We believe that by understanding the laws of nature and the order of the universe, we are getting closer to God in a meaningful way.

God serves as a moral compass in our lives. As we seek to understand the divine, we also seek to live according to ethical and moral principles that respect human dignity and promote the common good. Seeing God as a guiding presence helps us to make informed and ethical decisions in our lives.

In addition, God is a constant source of inspiration. Contemplating the beauty and complexity of nature fills us with awe and reverence. This awe inspires us to create, explore, innovate and seek the good in our world. We see human creativity as an extension of divine creativity.

The deistic view of God as a source of inspiration and guidance does not alienate us from the world, but involves us even more deeply in it. We value life and the human experience, finding meaning in daily interactions, personal achievements and the impact we can have on the world around us.

Our spirituality is not isolated, but integrated into everyday life. We constantly seek to understand the divine in our actions and in our quest for knowledge. We see God not as a distant spectator, but as a constant guide who motivates us to be better, to explore our connection with the cosmos and to contribute to the well-being of humanity.

Thus, the deistic vision of God as a source of inspiration and guidance is not just theoretical; it is a dynamic force that drives us to seek the truth, to live with integrity and to make a difference in the world. It is a constant call to authenticity, compassion and the search for divine knowledge in every aspect of existence.

Chapter 21
The Deist Philosophy in Practice

Deistic philosophy, my dear, is not limited to a set of abstract ideas, devoid of practical application. On the contrary, it is a philosophy that translates into actions and guidelines for our daily lives. As we explore how deistic principles and beliefs can be applied in practice, we find a philosophy that enriches and gives meaning to our existence.

Firstly, deism urges us to live authentically. We believe that understanding God as a creative and guiding force inspires us to be true to ourselves. We don't submit to rigid religious dogma or narrow interpretations of spirituality. Instead, we are encouraged to seek our own understanding of God and to live according to our personal convictions.

Moral autonomy is a fundamental pillar of deism. We believe that each individual possesses the ability to discern what is right and wrong on the basis of reason and ethics. This means that we are responsible for our actions and decisions. By applying this moral autonomy in daily life, we seek to act ethically, promoting justice and the well-being of all.

Deistic philosophy also invites us to constantly seek divine knowledge, and this search is not limited to temples or religious rituals. It is present in every moment of life. We value education, research and intellectual exploration as ways of getting closer to God. Understanding the natural world and the laws that govern it is seen as a way of revering divine creation.

Compassion and empathy are essential values. We believe that by understanding the interconnectedness of all life and the divine presence in every human being, we are called to treat others with compassion and respect. This understanding motivates us to actively seek ways to alleviate human suffering and promote the well-being of all.

Applying deistic philosophy in practice does not isolate us from the world; on the contrary, it involves us even more deeply in it. We are motivated to be agents of positive change in our community and in the world at large. We believe that by living according to our deistic principles, we contribute to building a more just, compassionate and harmonious world.

Thus, deism is not a passive philosophy, but a call to action. It is an approach to life that challenges us to live with integrity, to seek divine knowledge, to practice compassion and to work for the common good. It is a philosophy that transforms our daily existence into a journey of meaning and purpose.

The conception of God as an expression of universal mystery is a central element of deism, and this idea continues to inspire us and influence our spirituality. When we contemplate the universe and its vastness, we are reminded that there is something beyond our rational understanding, something that transcends our senses and knowledge.

In deism, we see God as the manifestation of this universal mystery. He is the creative principle behind everything that exists, the source of the order and beauty of the universe. Appreciation of this mystery invites us to a deep sense of reverence and humility before the grandeur of the cosmos.

At the same time, this vision of God as a universal mystery encourages us to seek knowledge and understanding. We believe that human reason is a precious gift that allows us to explore the natural world, uncover its secrets and understand the laws that govern it.

Furthermore, understanding God as an expression of the universal mystery reminds us of the interconnectedness of all things. Life on Earth is intrinsically linked to the universe, and every human being is part of this complex web of existence. This awareness motivates us to act responsibly towards the planet and all forms of life on it.

On a personal level, this vision of God as a universal mystery invites us to contemplation and meditation. We seek moments of stillness and reflection to connect with this divine presence that permeates the cosmos. These moments of contemplation help us find inner peace and deepen our connection with the divine.

Deist spirituality is a constant search to understand this universal mystery. We don't have rigid dogmas or prescribed rituals, but rather an open and exploratory approach to spirituality. Each person is encouraged to find their own way of connecting with God and exploring the divine mystery.

Our spirituality is marked by freedom and the individual search for truth. We value diversity of perspectives and beliefs, as we recognize that each person has a unique vision of the divine. This openness enriches us and allows us to learn from others.

God as an expression of the universal mystery inspires us to contemplate the grandeur of the cosmos, to seek divine knowledge, to act responsibly towards the Earth and to find peace in spiritual reflection. This vision motivates us to live with a deep sense of connection to the universe and to continually explore the mystery of existence.

As we move on to discuss the understanding of God in deism, it is crucial to consider how this vision aligns with the modern understanding of the cosmos and human existence. The modern era has brought with it significant advances in science, philosophy and the understanding of the universe, and deists have not been unaware of these transformations.

In the modern world, our understanding of the universe and nature has been enriched by science. Astronomy has revealed to us the vastness of the universe, with billions of galaxies and solar systems, challenging our previous understanding of the cosmos. However, this expansion of cosmic knowledge has not diminished the vision of God in deism; on the contrary, it has deepened our appreciation for the complexity and beauty of divine creation.

Advances in biology and the theory of evolution have also brought a new perspective on life on Earth. The realization that all living things share a common ancestor does not contradict the view of God as creator, but rather underscores the wonder of life's diversity and the interconnectedness of all life forms.

In the field of philosophy, modern thinkers such as Immanuel Kant and David Hume have influenced our understanding of God. Kant argued that the existence of God cannot be proven empirically, but that the idea of God is fundamental to morality and practical reason.

This approach resonates with deism, which sees reason as an essential tool for understanding God.

The view of God in deism also aligns with the modern emphasis on individual freedom and moral autonomy. Free will and personal responsibility are fundamental values, and deism values the human capacity to make ethical and moral choices based on reason and divine understanding.

The modern era has also brought advances in the understanding of human psychology, which can be related to the view of God in deism. Psychology teaches us about aspects of the human mind, including spirituality and the search for meaning. The view of God as a source of inspiration and guidance in everyday life fits well with the human search for purpose and spiritual connection.

Deism's understanding of God not only remains relevant in the modern age, but is also enriched by advances in scientific, philosophical and psychological knowledge. Deism continues to offer a vision of God that is coherent with contemporary understanding of the universe and human existence, maintaining its appeal as a meaningful spiritual approach for many.

For deists, God is not just a distant entity that created the universe, but a manifestation of the profound mystery that permeates all of existence.

The quest for divine knowledge in deism is ultimately a quest for understanding this universal mystery. It is a spiritual journey that leads us to explore the depths of the universe, both externally and internally. Through contemplation of nature and reflection on our own lives, we seek to unlock the secrets of the divine mystery.

Deistic spirituality values a direct connection with the universal mystery. We don't rely on religious intermediaries, rigid dogmas or prescribed rituals to bring us closer to God. Instead, we seek a personal and intimate relationship with the divine, allowing our own experience and understanding to guide our spiritual path.

Contemplation of nature and self-reflection are valued practices in deism, as they allow us to delve deeply into the universal mystery. By observing the grandeur of the universe and the complexity of life, we find inspiration for our own spiritual questions and reflections.

This perspective also pushes us to seek unity in diversity. By recognizing the universal mystery as a force that permeates all things, we are motivated to seek harmony, mutual understanding and respect for the beliefs of others. We see humanity as part of a greater whole and recognize the importance of working together in search of understanding and peace.

Chapter 22
God Beyond Space and Time

Allow me to lead you down the path of deep thought to explore a concept that is both challenging and fascinating: the nature of God in relation to space and time. As a master deist, it is my mission to guide you on this journey of reflection and contemplation.

Let's start by recognizing that our existence is intrinsically linked to a three-dimensional universe, where space and time are the coordinates that shape our understanding of reality. The world around us unfolds before us, from the darkness of the past to the mystery of the future. However, our view of the world is limited to these parameters, and it is at this point that we begin to wonder about the nature of God.

There is an invisible dimension, a reality beyond the reach of our physical senses and temporal logic. In this sphere, the laws that govern our three-dimensional universe do not apply. It is in this hidden realm that we can begin to glimpse the true essence of God.

As three-dimensional beings, we are confined to a reality that unfolds before our eyes, governed by the coordinates of space and time. However, the concept of God transcends these coordinates, and it is in this invisible dimension that He resides. Just as an inhabitant of a two-dimensional plane cannot perceive the third dimension, we three-dimensional beings are limited in our ability to understand what lies beyond space and time.

Of course, when I refer to an inhabitant of the second dimension, the mind quickly tries to associate the concept with something it can process, so it's important to point out that inhabitants of the second dimension are fictional. A classic example of an inhabitant of the second dimension can be found in the figure of a fictional being called a "Flatlander". Flatland is a book written by Edwin A. Abbott in 1884, which describes a two-dimensional world inhabited by flat figures. The characters in this world are simple polygons, such as squares, triangles and circles, who live on a two-dimensional plane, unable to perceive the existence of the third dimension.

The inhabitants of Flatland have no height, depth or ability to leave their plane. For them, everything that exists is contained within this two-dimensional reality. They can't look up or down, only forwards and backwards. Therefore, an inhabitant of Flatland is an example of a being who cannot perceive or understand the third dimension, just as we three-dimensional beings cannot directly perceive higher dimensions.

Having understood the concept of the second dimension, let's return to our own, because we live in a three-dimensional world, where the coordinates of space and time shape our reality and our understanding of the universe. However, when we turn to the nature of God, we are faced with an intriguing question: in which dimension does He reside? Some spiritual traditions suggest the existence of multiple dimensions beyond the three we perceive. Beings from the fourth, fifth or even higher dimensions are the subject of speculation in various philosophies. In this context, we can conclude that God belongs to an even higher and subtler dimension than the ones we conceive. This dimension transcends our three-dimensional limitations and is where the true divine essence can reside. Thus, when exploring the nature of God, we must consider the possibility that He dwells in a dimension beyond our comprehension, a spiritual realm that transcends the boundaries of space and time.

In this invisible realm, God is not just a distant figure, but a constant presence that transcends the physical rules of our three-dimensional world. He is the very essence of this dimension, a cosmic intelligence that is beyond our comprehension. Thus, the invisible dimension presents itself as a veil that conceals the totality of the divine mystery.

Still within this context of exploring the nature of God in relation to space and time, it is important to delve into the idea of an invisible dimension that houses the divine. It's as if we were facing an intricate cosmic puzzle, and the next piece we should examine is the idea of the cosmic web.

Imagine the universe as a vast interconnected web, where each strand represents a part of existence. This web covers everything from the most distant star systems to the atoms that make up our bodies. In this context, we are like little interconnected fragments of this universal web, each with our own experience and consciousness, but each doing our part in the whole.

Now consider that God is the supreme weaver of this cosmic web. He not only created it, but also sustains it. Every thread, every connection, is part of His great work. However, at the same time as being intrinsically linked to every aspect of the web, God transcends the web itself.

This metaphor allows us to understand how God is omnipresent, being everywhere at once, while remaining beyond the reach of our three-dimensional perception. Just as the weaver deeply understands the web he has created, God knows every aspect of the universe he sustains.

Furthermore, the cosmic web helps us to understand how our own individual journeys are interconnected. Each choice we make, each experience we live through, is like a thread that intertwines with the others. God, as the master weaver, weaves these threads together in harmony, creating a pattern that transcends our limited understanding.

Now, we must turn to the intrinsic mystery of existence. As deists, we understand that God is the beginning of all things, the creator of the universe and of time. However, this understanding does not prevent us from recognizing the profound enigma that surrounds existence itself.

Existence is a vast ocean of infinite possibilities, where each point is a moment in time and space. Now consider that God is the source of this ocean, the origin of all possibilities. Every event, every choice, is like a ripple in that ocean, affecting all the other ripples.

In this context, God not only created the universe, but is also the very essence of reality. He is the core of every atom, the force behind every event, and the cause of every effect. At the same time, however, God is much more than the sum of all the parts. He is the mystery that permeates all of existence, the enigma that challenges us to explore more deeply.

As we contemplate this mystery, we are reminded of our ongoing quest for divine knowledge. As an integral part of the cosmic web, each of us has the capacity to understand God's nature more deeply. By exploring the mystery of existence, we are drawing closer to God, even if His transcendent essence remains beyond our comprehension.

The modern understanding of evolution, both of the universe and of life on Earth, is a manifestation of the divine plan. The development of human consciousness and critical thinking skills is also considered an intrinsic part of the spiritual journey.

Our understanding of the cosmos and human existence is constantly evolving, as is our understanding of God. Deists see God as the eternal principle behind these discoveries, a God who not only created the universe, but also gave us the ability to explore and understand it.

Universal mystery refers to the realization that there are aspects of the cosmos and human existence that are beyond our ability to comprehend. Even with all the scientific and philosophical advances, there are elements of reality that remain enigmatic and challenging.

The universal mystery reminds us that although we can make remarkable discoveries and advance our understanding, there will always be more to learn and explore. Humility in the face of this mystery encourages us to remain open to knowledge, reflection and the ongoing search for God.

Chapter 23
The Nature of the Soul in Deism

The soul is perceived as a divine spark, the immortal essence that transcends the physical body. This view of the soul differs from many other religious traditions that associate the soul with a destiny of rewards or punishments after death, because for deists, the immortality of the soul is intrinsic to its nature.

It is crucial to understand that, for deists, the soul is not a separate entity from God, but rather an extension of this immaterial and transcendental divinity. We believe that the soul is a spark of divine consciousness that resides in every human being, a fundamental part of our existence that connects us to the primordial essence of the universe and to God himself.

This perspective of the soul as immortal and its deep relationship with the physical body inspires deists to value every moment of earthly life. We see life as a precious opportunity for spiritual growth and self-knowledge, as every action, thought and choice has a lasting impact on the soul's journey.

As we reflect on the nature of the soul in Deism, I invite us to consider the deeper meaning of existence. The soul is the anchor of our connection with the divine, the light that guides us towards transcendence. It is the constant reminder that we are part of something greater.

The soul is not a static entity, but a constantly evolving being. During earthly life, the soul undergoes a profound and significant transformation. This transformation takes place as we learn, grow and face the challenges of existence.

Earthly experience is the soul's workshop, a place where we face tribulations and joys, successes and failures. Each experience shapes our soul, contributing to our spiritual growth. Pain teaches us compassion, adversity strengthens us, and love connects us to the divine spark that dwells within us.

It is important to understand that although the soul is immortal, it is not immune to the influences of the material world. Our journey is like a school, a place of learning where the soul accumulates wisdom and experience. The transformation of the soul involves the assimilation of these lessons and the resulting spiritual evolution.

The relationship between the physical body and the soul plays a fundamental role in this transformation.

The body serves as the container that allows the soul to interact with the material world. As we live our lives, the soul absorbs the impressions and experiences of the body, and this interaction is fundamental to our growth.

It is through the choices we make, the ethical decisions we take and the experiences we accumulate that the soul evolves. The transformation of the soul is not a passive process, but an effort to become more aware, more compassionate and closer to God.

Understanding the transformation of the soul leads us to a deeper appreciation of our earthly journey. Every challenge we face, every obstacle we overcome, contributes to our spiritual growth. In this way, earthly life becomes a precious opportunity for the soul to grow and develop.

When considering the nature of the soul in Deism, it is essential to highlight the ultimate purpose of this spiritual journey. Deists believe that, after its spiritual evolution and search for divine knowledge, the soul is destined to achieve transcendence.

Transcendence, for deists, is the supreme state of communion with God. It is the ultimate realization of the soul's spiritual journey, where it merges completely with divinity. In this state, the soul understands the true nature of God and experiences profound spiritual unity and peace.

The journey towards transcendence is an incessant search for truth and connection with the divine. It involves intellectual exploration, self-reflection, the continuous search for divine knowledge and the practice of ethical and moral values. It is a journey that challenges the mind and nourishes the soul, leading to a deeper understanding of oneself, the universe and God.

When the soul reaches transcendence, it ceases to be a separate entity from God and becomes an inseparable part of divinity. This union is the culmination of the deist's spiritual quest, where individuality dissolves in the presence of God. It is a state of fullness and spiritual enlightenment that surpasses any verbal description.

Chapter 24
Contribution to Human History

In human history, Deism has played a significant role, particularly during the so-called "Age of Reason". This historical period, which stretched from the end of the 17th century to the 18th century, was marked by a fervent advance in human thought, driven by the pursuit of reason, science and philosophy. Deism emerged as a response to many of the religious dogmas of the time and established itself as a philosophy that promoted freedom of thought, reason and the search for an independent understanding of God.

During the Age of Reason, influential thinkers such as John Locke, Voltaire and Thomas Paine began to challenge traditional conceptions of religion and defend the belief in a deistic God.

Deism left an indelible mark on human history, influencing not only intellectual development, but also social and political transformation in various parts of the world.

The French Revolution, which took place between 1789 and 1799, was one of the most emblematic moments in world history, marking a radical transformation in the political and social structure of France and having a lasting impact on the whole world. Deism played a notable role in this period of change and upheaval.

The principles of liberty, equality and fraternity, pillars of the French Revolution, were in tune with the ideals of many deists of the time. Figures such as Maximilien Robespierre and Jacques Hébert, who were sympathetic to Deism, played prominent roles in the Revolution, promoting ideas of secularism, separation of church and state and a more rational approach to religion.

Deism also influenced the Civil Constitution of the Clergy, promulgated in 1790, which placed the Catholic Church under state control, reducing its power. Deists saw organized religion as an obstacle to freedom of thought and the search for truth, and the French Revolution provided the opportunity to make significant changes in this field. In addition, the French Revolution had a global impact, inspiring emancipation movements and struggles for rights all over the world.

Another hallmark of Deism was the Enlightenment, an intellectual movement that swept Europe during the 17th and 18th centuries, emphasizing the power of reason, science and education to improve society. Deism was intrinsically linked to this period of enlightenment, contributing to the development of progressive and secular ideas.

Deist philosophers such as Voltaire, Rousseau and Diderot produced works that questioned religious institutions and defended freedom of thought and expression. Their criticism of revealed religions and their support for a more abstract and universal God profoundly influenced Enlightenment thinking.

The Encyclopédie, one of the greatest achievements of the Enlightenment, was contributed to by many notable deists. Diderot, the work's editor-in-chief, and other contributors, used this platform to disseminate deistic ideas to promote secular education. The Encyclopédie advocated a more rational view of the world and knowledge, and its pages were a vehicle for challenging religious dogmatism.

Deism also had a significant impact on the intellectual and political revolutions of the time. The ideals of liberty, equality and fraternity that emerged during the Enlightenment were partly influenced by notions of a God who created humanity as equals and endowed them with reason.

The legacy of Deism in human history is profound and lasting. Its intellectual and philosophical contributions have shaped the way many people perceive God, spirituality and the relationship between religion and reason. Many of the principles defended by deists, such as freedom of thought, the search for truth through reason and the separation of religion and government, are still fundamental to today's democracies and pluralistic societies.

Deism has also influenced the emergence of more open and inclusive spiritual and religious currents. Many people, in search of a spirituality that embraces freedom of belief and reason, find in Deism a philosophy that resonates with their values.

In addition, Deism has played an important role in promoting religious tolerance and the acceptance of different spiritual viewpoints. Its emphasis on a universal and impersonal God has allowed people to move away from sectarian divisions and embrace a more inclusive view of spirituality.

One of Deism's most notable contributions to recent history was its influence on the founding of the United States of America. The founders of the American nation were strongly influenced by Deism and incorporated Deistic principles into important national documents.

The Declaration of Independence, drafted mainly by Thomas Jefferson, includes references to the "Law of Nature and Nature's God," a deistic conception of a God who governs the universe through natural laws. Jefferson, who was a deist, defended the separation of church and state and believed that individuals had inalienable rights conferred by the Creator, but without association to a specific organized religion.

The United States Constitution, with its amendment prohibiting the establishment of an official religion, also reflects the deist influence. The drafters of the constitutional text recognized the importance of protecting religious freedom and allowing citizens to practice their beliefs without government interference.

The influence of Deism on the founding of the United States is evident in the vision of a limited government, based on rational laws, that does not impose specific religious beliefs on citizens. This approach reflects the principles of liberty, equality and tolerance that were dear to the Deists of the time.

Deism therefore not only shaped philosophical and religious thought, but also had a tangible impact on the structure and politics of one of the world's most influential nations. Its legacy continues to be felt in the civil liberties and separation of religion and government that are fundamental to American democracy and many other democratic nations around the world. Deism is undoubtedly the philosophy that transcends the ages and continues to inspire those who seek to understand the divine in a freer and more reflective way.

Chapter 25
Famous Deists

History has been positively impacted by the actions of brilliant minds who, at some point, shared their deeds and philosophies with humanity. It is undeniable that these exceptional minds would not submit to pre-established dogmas. Behind religious conceptions imposed by force or conviction, intriguing stories were hidden, machinations that would challenge even the most daring strategists. It is well known that practically all religious currents have their blemishes and contradictions, which makes it understandable that brilliant minds would seek a conception of God more compatible with their remarkable intellectual abilities.

In this context, several personalities emerged as propagators of Deism, a religious philosophy that managed to harmonize the creative minds of these unique figures with spirituality. These notable thinkers and their visions of a Deistic God include:

Isaac Newton (1643/1727): The English physicist and mathematician is considered one of humanity's greatest geniuses. The formulator of the laws of classical mechanics, universal gravitation and differential and integral calculus, Newton also dedicated himself to the study of optics, astronomy, alchemy and theology. His belief in a God who created the universe with order and harmony, but who did not interfere in human affairs, shaped his worldview.

Voltaire (1694/1778): The French philosopher and writer was one of the main exponents of the Enlightenment. An advocate of freedom of expression, religious tolerance, scientific progress and the fight against superstition, Voltaire criticized revealed religions such as Christianity, Judaism and Islam. He defended the existence of a God who was the first cause of everything, but who was not involved in earthly matters.

Thomas Jefferson (1743/1826): The American politician and statesman, principal author of the United States Declaration of Independence, was also an architect, inventor, agronomist and naturalist. Jefferson embraced rationalist deism, which rejected miracles, the divinity of Jesus and the inspiration of the scriptures. For him, God was the creator of natural laws, but did not directly interfere in human history.

Benjamin Franklin (1706/1790): An American scientist and diplomat, Franklin was one of the leaders of the American Revolution and contributed to various fields, including physics, electricity, meteorology, medicine and biology. He was also a journalist, editor, writer, philanthropist and abolitionist. As a pragmatic deist, Franklin saw God as the source of morality and virtue, without the need for specific religious rituals.

Albert Einstein (1879/1955): German physicist and philosopher, Einstein revolutionized modern physics with the theory of general relativity and contributed to several other areas, including quantum mechanics, cosmology, statistics and the philosophy of science. He was awarded the Nobel Prize for Physics in 1921. Einstein was a pantheistic deist, who saw God as a manifestation of the beauty and intelligence inherent in the universe.

John Locke (1632/1704): English philosopher known for his contributions to political philosophy and the theory of knowledge. Locke believed in a God who granted natural rights to individuals, including liberty and private property. His ideas directly influenced the founders of the United States.

Ethan Allen (1738/1789): One of the founders of the state of Vermont and leader of the militia known as the "Green Mountain Boys." Allen was a deist and author of the book "Reason, the Only Oracle of Mankind." His ideas influenced political and religious thought in the United States.

Ethan Allen Hitchcock (1798/1870): American military man, explorer and author, known for his expeditions to the American West. Hitchcock was a deist who believed in God as the Creator and, at the same time, questioned organized religions.

Thomas Paine (1737/1809): Anglo-American writer and philosopher, author of "Common Sense" and "The Rights of Man". Paine defended Deism and religious freedom, believing that religion should be a personal matter, not imposed by the state.

John Adams (1735/1826): One of the Founding Fathers of the United States as a nation and the country's second president. Adams was a deist who believed in a creator God, but also criticized the dogmatic interpretations of organized religions.

Ralph Waldo Emerson (1803/1882): American philosopher, essayist and poet associated with the transcendentalist movement. Emerson promoted an individualistic and unconventional spirituality, influenced by Deism and Eastern thought.

Henry David Thoreau (1817/1862): American writer, poet and philosopher, famous for his book "Walden" and his essay "Civil Disobedience". Thoreau was a deist who valued a direct connection with nature and the search for spiritual truth.

Acknowledgements

At this crucial point in the journey through Deism, I would like to express deep gratitude to you, the dedicated reader, who has followed this exploration of the ideas, principles and philosophy that underpin this unique worldview.

We thank you for your unwavering curiosity, your thirst for knowledge and your commitment to understanding the complexities of Deism. We know that exploring philosophical and spiritual concepts can often be challenging, but you persisted.

Just as the pioneers of Deism challenged traditional narratives and proposed a deeper understanding of divinity, you dedicated yourself to exploring these ideas with an open mind and heart. Your search for truth through reason and critical thinking echoes the fundamental principles of Deism.

Thank you for being part of this conversation and for contributing to the collective understanding of Deism. We hope that this exploration has enriched your own spiritual and intellectual journey.

Our hearts are filled with gratitude for your presence and engagement in this quest to understand the divine through reason and observation. May your journey continue to be illuminated by the light of wisdom and understanding.

With sincere gratitude,

Team Luan Ferr.

www.ingramcontent.com/pod-product-compliance
Lightning Source LLC
LaVergne TN
LVHW040058080526
838202LV00045B/3705